The Proof is
in the Pudding

Second Edition

Fundraiser for:

Community Service Center of Northern Champaign County
520 E. Wabash Ave, Suite #1
Rantoul, IL 61866
Phone: 217-893-1530

Your First Call for Help

*   *   *

The Proof is in the Pudding

Mary Margaret Kruger

To order additional copies of this book, contact:
Xlibris Corporation
1-888-795-4274
www.Xlibris.com
Orders@Xlibris.com
57045

Contents

"The Proof is in the Pudding"

is being dedicated to the Community Service Center of Northern Champaign County and to all the wonderful people who continue to keep *HOPE* alive in these communities. The services offered by the CSC would not be possible without the forty plus wonderful and dedicated volunteers as well as the many food and financial donations that come into the CSC from groups and individuals through-out the entire year. All proceeds for this book go directly to the Community Service Center of Northern Champaign County.

God Bless You—One and All!

*   *   *

Special Thanks
to the CSC Staff and Board of Directors

Executive Director—Andy Kulczycki
Service Coordinator—Karen Kelly
Secretary/Bookkeeper—Sharon Thompson
Office Assistant & Community Case Manager—Wendy Hundley

Board President—Mary Kruger
Vice President—Dan Grieser
Treasurer—Gwen McMorris
Secretary—Brenda Crane
Benjamin Cheek
Carolyn Jones
Fred Meek
Brian Schurter
Herbert Taylor
John Vasquez

Acknowledgements

Okay ~ so this isn't your typical acknowledgement. In all fairness ~ this is not your typical recipe book either. With that in mind I would like to acknowledge some truths of my existence—lending to the important facts of why publishing this book as well as helping the Community Service Center has been so dear to my heart.

Just as each recipe in this book is different so it is with each of our lives. We may have eaten similar foods growing up but the environment we lived in fed our souls on entirely different levels.

Many of the ingredients in my life were bitter-sweet. I grew up on a farm which I dearly loved—but I was in a home where violence and abuse was on the daily menu. I was constantly being fried and re-fried with verbal insults—deflating what little self esteem I did have.

My childhood could easily be compared to that of a loaf of bread that was prepared with bad yeast. Anyone who has baked bread from scratch knows that to have good yeast it must be prepared in a luke-warm base. Not hot—not cold; but comfortably in the middle. Otherwise the bread cannot grow—any more than a child can rise to his or her fullest potential.

Raising a child—like working yeast takes time, patience and a warm heart. Once a child begins to grow there will be some "air bubbles" along the way that need to be worked out—but they certainly do not have to be beaten out. Gentle but firm kneading is quite effective. Now—do keep in mind—getting all the "air pockets" out is next to impossible and that is okay. Neither child nor loaf of bread was meant to be perfect.

Children who have been abused often seek out friends and partners who are abusive or hold similar behaviors. The father of my children was not a bad person any more than my father was. He just made some choices that were not healthy for me or my children to live with. So after 21 years of marriage and nine children I wound up a divorced—single mom.

But with the help and support of a great community and some really awesome counselors I was able to break that cycle and find my own recipe for life. It wasn't easy being a single parent and turning things around, but my children were my number one priority and I was willing to do whatever it took to give them the life they deserved.

I leaned on the Community Service Center and local food pantry in Watseka Illinois where I lived at the time to help me transition into a better life. That support became the turning point of my life and a time I will long remember and be eternally grateful for. That help gave me hope. Publishing this book is just a small way for me to pay-it-forward.

The proof is truly in the pudding—community is very important! With time, patience and the right ingredients anything is possible. I raised nine very beautiful, intelligent children to become wonderfully healthy productive adults—but I could not have done it alone. My blessings now include nine adorable grandchildren, an outstanding husband, four step-children and a step-grandson.

People often assume food bank customers are homeless or helpless and stupid. But many are actually very intelligent—working class people who have met up with a few challenges. Some have had to give up buying groceries so that they can pay rent or put gas in their car. Others have serious disabilities rendering them incapable of maintaining the physical or mental demands of daily employment. No matter what their needs—God blesses the giver. So whether you purchased one of these recipe books or helped in defraying the cost to print them or just shared a recipe or simple hug of encouragement—I am eternally grateful. You are my community family. Your support really does make difference.

~ God Bless ~

Editor/Publisher/Author

Mary Kruger

Overallmom53@hotmail.com

"I shall pass through this world but once. Any good therefore that I can do or any kindness that I can show to any human being, let me do it now. Let me not defer or neglect it, for I shall not pass this way again."
—Mahatma Gandhi

Introduction

Life is so much easier when we are a part of a community—a network of family and friends. Community is the village, the neighborhood, the church, that place where people look out for each other and support each other, where joys and sorrows, good times and bad times are shared.

"The Proof is in the Pudding" is about community. A booklet filled with delicious recipes and seasoned with stories of just a few of the many wonderful people from this community of life.

Each chapter of this book is dedicated to a different area of community; from my personal family, to the many area churches, to my work family, the CSC volunteer network of friends and so on.

The recipes in this book have been donated by members of my personal family as well as my community family. And below you will see a list of several items the center is in great need of and would appreciate your help with.

*   *   *

Community Service Center ~ Wish List ~

Digital Camera
Laptop Computer
Bathroom Facelift
Electric Stove
Folding Tables & Stacking Chairs
Cart for Storing Tables & Chairs
Brochure Rack
Storage Shelves
Wall Mounted Corner TV Shelf

8' Counter with Storage Below

* * * On Going Needs * * *

Nonperishable Foods
Diapers & Toilet Paper, etc.

Personal Hygiene Items

Dish Soap & Laundry Detergent
Board Games—(Rantoul Area Project—Youth Program)

It seems only fitting that I should begin this book with a true story about a family whose main ingredient for life is their faith. In order to live and survive in this world we need more than just food for our bodies; we need nourishment for our souls as well. The Thomas Hall family is just one family amongst many in our community that shines with the faith to survive insurmountable odds. It was this story that rekindled my faith and motivated me to get back to my writing. With this column (Rantoul Press—1/21/04) I have written/published close to 200 columns and now this—my first book. Although Tom and his wife have since moved from the Rantoul area their inspiration lives on in the hearts of many.

Miracle on Borman Street

No—that's not 34th Street! But yes, it certainly is a Christmas story to long be remembered.

December 1, 2003, Thomas Hall of Rantoul was declared clinically dead for 42 minutes due to a massive heart attack he suffered following one of his routine walks. But today he lives to tell his story.

It was a bitter cold day that Monday morning when Thomas decided to take his daily two mile walk inside the shelter and protection of the Forum Fitness Center in Rantoul, Illinois. Most days Tom could be seen walking around town while taking photos of the sights; whether it be of new construction or old structures his camera was in tow. But this day was different. The only pictures he would have would be the flash-backs of what could have been a terrible tragedy.

Leaving the Fitness Center after his work out Tom climbed into his pickup truck and headed for home going north on Enterprise Street. Meanwhile Officer Casagrande, who just happened to be driving east on Borman Street, noticed the Hall pickup driving erratically and without warning veer off the road into a building at the corner of Enterprise and Borman. Officer Saltsgaver, who also just happened to be in the area, rushed to assist Casagrande in freeing Tom from his locked vehicle enabling them to administer CPR.

As Thomas was rushed by ambulance to the Hospital one of the officers phoned Toms wife, Marilyn, to inform her there had been an accident. Within minutes she and her children were on their way to the hospital. Upon the families arrival they were told that Tom's heart was gone and that there was no brain activity. Medically there was nothing more doctors could do.

Devastated by the news yet trusting this was God's will the family began saying their goodbyes.

Meanwhile Tom's other daughter, Kathy, who upon receiving the news began racing home from Indiana praying frantically that God give her one last chance to talk to her father.

Kathy made a point of calling home every day, sometimes only speaking to her mother and other days talking with both parents. But this day she had yet to make that call.

Back at the hospital Susan bent down to kiss her father for what she believed to be the last time—when suddenly there was life. Thomas lifted his hand to his forehead, touching the exact spot where he had just been kissed, creating quite an emotional race for doctors and staff. The doctors immediately began the process to surgically implant a stint in order to keep Tom's heart pumping.

In spite of a 90% blockage and the bottom half of his heart being blown out Thomas was back in church that following Sunday, just as he had been the day before his accident. His only loss was a bit of short term memory and the donuts he was bringing home for breakfast that bitter sweet Monday morning.

From the moment news went out to family and friends about the accident prayers were ringing through the heavens from as far away as California, and Florida, to Oklahoma, Wisconsin, Tennessee, and of course through out Indiana and Illinois.

"It was a miracle from answered prayer," Tom's daughter Kathy said. And I personally could not agree more.

God Bless the Thomas Hall family. Your faith shines on. There was more than one heart brought back to life that day. ~

*   *   *

"We can do no great things—only small things
with great love." ~ Mother Teresa

The recipes in this "family" section came from my nine children, their partners and or spouses, my husband, his kids and of course I sprinkled a few of my own in as well. ~ Enjoy!

The Family That Eats Together—Stays Together

Each morning all nine of my children would gather around the kitchen table for breakfast. They took turns preparing that meal by the week. Cold cereal was only allowed one morning of their stint. The rest of the days were their choice of pan-cakes, French toast, hot cereal, eggs, or whatever else their creative minds could come up with.

Yes—it took some organization and sharing of two bathrooms to get everyone off to school and or work on time, and those were crazy times. But it was worth every minute of it. To this day with all my children on their own—and my baby now 24 years old with two children of her own—any one of them would tell you that breakfast is still their favorite meal.

Now grant it—at the time those kids were getting up early and/or preparing that breakfast they would not have agreed. But now as adults they treasure the numerous memories that came from being around that table as a family.

According to recent surveys, less than half of the families in the United States actually sit down to a meal on a regular basis. Yet, studies report that family meals are strongly related to the development of adolescent mental health and stability.

A Harvard Medical School study found that there are nutritional, as well as social, emotional and academic advantages that take place in children when families share meals together.

Keep in mind that if you are too busy to have family meals, then quite possibly you may be too busy. So plan ahead, be creative and make adjustments to fit your family's schedule.

It's important to have mealtimes without television or other distractions. Keep food simple and varied but serve family members the same food at the same time. Limit table discussion to agreeable or neutral topics focusing on the positive. Let the children get involved in planning and preparing as well as serving the meals.

Most importantly teach your child by showing. When you make pleasant family meal times a priority, your child will more likely be healthy, well-mannered and well-adjusted.

It's a recipe that's proven to be successful!

*   *   *

Children are like wet cement. Whatever falls on them makes an impression. ~ Haim Ginott

Stephanie's famous fried chicken happens to be a recipe that has been handed down through the generations. Her great-grandmother Grace Denault taught her daughter-in-law Connie Denault (my mother), who taught me and I Stephanie—how to fry chicken using this method. I added the step of baking the chicken to give it added flavor and tenderness. Stephanie enjoyed the chicken so much she followed suit adding parsley flakes to garnish.

Country Fry-Baked Chicken

(Daughter & 1st Born) Stephanie Gadbois
Stephanie and her two sons live in Normal, Illinois

1-Whole chicken cleaned and cut into pieces (or package of chicken pieces of choice)

*All you need is your *chicken*, enough *flour* to coat chicken, *salt & pepper*, *oil* for frying, a *brown paper sack* and *parsley flakes*.

Begin by putting one cup (more for bigger quantities of meat) of flour mixed with salt and pepper to season into a (clean) brown paper sack. Then place your fresh clean chicken parts (legs, wings, thighs, whatever) into the bag with the flour mix. Roll bag down a couple times to close and hold shut as you gently shake and move the chicken parts around coating each piece as evenly as possible.

In a hot skillet or fry pan pour ½ cup (plus or minus) of canola oil. When oil is hot gently shake excess flour off each piece of chicken and place in hot grease. Turn heat to a medium setting. You want oil hot enough to brown the meat but not burn it. Once each side of your meat is crisp and nicely browned place each piece of meat in a greased baking dish. Do not stack or crowd the pieces of meat.

Sprinkle with a little more salt if you'd like and bake in the oven at 350 degrees for 35 to 45 minutes. Before serving Stephanie likes to sprinkle fresh parsley flakes over the chicken as a garnish.

Green Beans Deluxe

Mary's sister—Wanda Warman
Owner of Nana's Cakery, Bradley IL
www.nanascakery.com

1-pound of bacon (cut into pieces)
1-medium size onion (diced)
½ cup sugar
1/4 cup vinegar
2-cans green beans (drained)

Fry bacon pieces until they start to get crispy; add onions and continue to fry for a few minutes. Add sugar and vinegar on medium/low heat—cooking until mix is clear. About 10 minutes. Add beans and stir together. Let simmer for a few minutes and serve immediately.

Josh's Baked Tilapia

(Son—2nd Child) Joshua Gadbois
Raleigh, NC

6 Tilapia filets (better if fresh not frozen)
2 eggs
1/4 cup butter (soft or melted)
½ cup crumbled corn flakes
1/4 cup parmesan cheese (shredded—same as you would use for spaghetti)

Additional spices to taste: Cayenne pepper, Italian seasoning, pinch of garlic, salt & pepper

Preheat oven to 375 degrees. Spray cooking oil on cookie sheet. Beat 2 eggs in bowl by itself.—Mix the rest of the ingredients in another slightly larger bowl (minus the filets). Dip the tilapia filets into the beaten eggs, and then dip into other bowl with remainder of ingredients. Lay battered filets on to cookie sheet (if any dry mixture left cover filets with it)

Bake at 375 degrees for 15 minutes. Let cool for 5 minutes then commence the feast!!!!!!

Morning Glory Muffins—(Quite delicious and healthy)

Momma—Mary Kruger
Rantoul, IL

2-cups flour
1-1/4 cup sugar
2-teaspoons Baking Soda
2-teaspoons Cinnamon
½ teaspoon salt

½ cup oil
½ cup applesauce
3-eggs—lightly beaten
2-teaspoon vanilla

2-cups grated peeled apples
½ cup raisins and/or dried cranberries
½ cup coconut
½ cup shredded carrots
½ cup chopped walnuts

Mix all dry ingredients together in one dish. In another bowl mix oil, applesauce, eggs, and vanilla; stir into dry ingredients. In separate dish combine grated apples, raisins, coconut, shredded carrots and chopped walnuts; stir and fold into other mixture. Fill greased or paper filled muffin tins 2/3 full and Bake at 350 degrees for 25-30 minutes. Makes 1-½ dozen muffins; stays fresh for a full week and does not need to be refrigerated.

Mexican Fiesta Ole!!!

Joshua's Fiancé—Eliza Maria Diaz-Williamson
Raleigh, NC

A Yummy Treat and fun to fix and eat!!! Ready in 30! Baby got Burrito and GuacamOLE!

Guacamole:

1-package of McCormick Great Guacamole (Eliza prefer Mild)
4-Avocados
½ lime
2-shakes of Garlic salt
2-tomatoes
1-bag of tortilla chips

Mix: Avocados; remove pits and peel, Mash pulp with spoon or potato masher. Add McCormick Mix, garlic and squeeze ½ lime. Finally add diced tomatoes and refrigerate for 30 min. So good!! Eat it up yum!!

Burrito:

1-pound of Ground Beef
1-packet of McCormick Taco Seasoning Mix
1-½ small white onion
1-can of Goya Black Beans (the best beans EVER!)
1-cloves of Garlic
1-can of low sodium chicken broth
2-tomatos
1-package of shredded Mexican cheese
sour cream (preference)
2-Tablespoons of Olive Oil
1-package of flower tortillas

Beans :

Sauté diced onions and olive oil in pot over medium heat. Stir occasionally. After onions are soft, add diced garlic and cook for 2 minutes. Then add chicken broth and can of Goya Black Beans. Let chicken broth cook on medium to low heat. Stir occasionally.

Beef:

Cook ground beef, drain, add package of seasoning with water (as directed on back of package). Dice tomatoes for topping. After beans are done place beef, beans, and all other fixings on flower tortillas and enjoy!

Reheats wonderfully! Everything is even better the next day!

Strawberry Preserve Cupcakes

(Daughter & 3rd Child)Veronica Gadbois
North Carolina

1-package strawberry cake mix
2-cups sour cream
3-eggs
1/4 cup water
1/3 cup strawberry preserves
2-muffin pans and 24 baking cups

Preheat oven to 350 degrees and put cups in muffin pans. Then stir together cake mix, sour cream, eggs and water until blended. Fill muffin cups ½ way with batter. Spoon ½ teaspoon of the preserves in the center of each cup. Top off cup with batter to 3/4. Bake for 20-30 minutes. Cool for one minute then remove from pan. Ice when cooled.

[Veronica says cream cheese white icing is great on these cupcakes. She dresses them up with red sugar sprinkles too. "They smell so good and the color just makes you smile!" says Veronica.]

Cream Cheese Icing

8-ounces cream cheese
½ cup butter or margarine

2-cups powdered sugar
1-teaspoon vanilla extract

Mix until creamy and ice cool cake. (Rhiannon Hogards' Recipe)

Zucchini Bread

(Daughter & 4th Child) Jessica Gadbois
Sacramento, CA

3-cups all-purpose flour
1-teaspoon salt
1-teaspoon baking soda
1-teaspoon baking powder
2-teaspoons ground cinnamon
3-eggs
1-cup vegetable oil
2-1/4 cups white sugar
3-teaspoons vanilla extract
2-cups grated zucchini
½ cup chopped walnuts

Grease and flour two—8 x 4 inch pans. Preheat oven to 325 degrees F. Sift flour, salt, baking powder, soda, and cinnamon together in a bowl. Beat eggs, oil, vanilla, and sugar together in a large bowl. Add sifted ingredients to the creamed mixture, and beat well. Stir in zucchini and nuts until well combined. Pour batter into prepared pans. Bake for 40 to 60 minutes. Cool in pan on rack for 20 minutes.

Cremini Mushrooms

Jessica Gadbois and her two daughters live in Sacramento, CA
(This is Jessica's original recipe for preparing Cremini Mushrooms)

1-pound fresh Cremini mushrooms (sliced and cleaned)
½ cup of butter (1 stick, cold, sliced)
2-diced cloves of garlic
2-Tablespoons of your favorite beer (can use non-alcohol too)
Salt/Pepper/Lawry's Seasoning salt—to taste

Melt about 1/4 cup of butter on med-low heat; drop in diced garlic until slightly browning.

Add diced mushrooms and beer, season to taste. Add rest of butter as the mushrooms start to cook down, or skip for less saucy mushrooms. Cook until tender, season as you stir. Enjoy!!

Taffy Apple Mix

(Son & 5th child)—Jeremiah Gadbois (Ashkum, IL) brought this home from school when he was 10 years old. He is now married to Devon and they have 3 children.

1-(8 ounce) package cream cheese softened
1/4 cup white sugar
3/4 cup brown sugar
1-teaspoon vanilla
1-cup salted peanuts—chopped fine
2-apples sliced

Mix cheese, sugars, vanilla, and nuts together well. Dip sliced apples into mix and eat away!

White Sangria

(Daughter & 6th child) Sarah Gadbois
Chicago, IL

½ cup peach schnapps
½ cup cognac
1/4 cup white sugar
4-oranges, sliced into rounds
2-mangos, peeled and sliced
4-(750 milliliter) bottles dry white wine, chilled
1-liter ginger ale, chilled

In a pitcher, combine peach schnapps, cognac, sugar, sliced oranges and sliced mangos. Chill for at least an hour. Pour fruit mixture into a large punch bowl. Stir in white wine and ginger ale.

---

*Momma's note: What can I say? I asked my kids to send one of their favorite recipes!!

Sausage Bread

(Daughter & 7th child) Theresa (Gadbois) Swaim
Waukee, Iowa

1-loaf of bread dough (if frozen thaw but do not let rise)
8-ounces cooked sausage
8-ounces mozzarella cheese
½ cup parmesan cheese
1-Tablespoon oregano
2-cloves of garlic finely chopped
1-stick melted butter or margarine

Roll out homemade bread dough to about 1/4 inch thickness. Brush with melted butter then layer the remaining ingredients. Roll dough from the long edge slowly and tightly keeping all ingredients together. Place on greased baking sheet and bake at 350 degrees until dough takes on a golden brown luster—about 20-25 minutes. Remove from oven, slice and serve as is or with a marinara sauce. [When Theresa first made this bread for her siblings they attacked it liked vultures—leaving Theresa to scavenge for crumbs.]

Mustachio Italiano

Joe Swaim (Theresa's husband)
Waukee, Iowa

1-pound package Mustachio, uncooked
1-pound Italian sausage or lean ground beef (cooked and drained)
2-jars pasta sauce (12 oz)
4-cups shredded Mozzarella Cheese
chopped parsley

Cook pasta, drain, preheat oven to 350 degrees. In a large bowl combine noodles, meat, pasta sauce and 2 cups cheese, mix well. Spoon into a greased 13x19 inch baking dish and cover; bake 45 minutes or until hot and bubbly. Uncover and top with remaining 2 cups cheese and parsley, bake 10 minutes longer or until cheese is melted. Makes 8 servings

Sloppy Joes

(Son & 8th child) Joseph Gadbois
Wilmington, NC

2 pounds ground beef—browned and drained
1-medium onion diced
3-Tablespoons classic mustard—(not dry mustard)
1-cup catsup (more or less according to taste)
2-Tablespoons brown sugar
Hamburger Buns

After meat is browned and drained stir in onions and cook until tender; add mustard, catsup, brown sugar and simmer for 20 minutes. Serve on hamburger buns or baked potatoes with sour cream and cheese. [Joseph always enjoyed eating sloppy Joes but really disliked what they were called and thought the name should be changed.)

Carolina Baked Beans & Pork Chops

(Daughter & 9th child) Margaret Leonetti
Lutz, FL

2-(16 ounce) cans pork & beans
½ cup chopped onions
½ cup chopped green bell pepper
1/4 cup yellow mustard
1/4 cup packed light brown sugar
2-Tablespoons Worcestershire Sauce
1-Tablespoon Cayenne Pepper Sauce
6-boneless pork chops (1 inch thick or smaller)

Preheat oven to 400 degrees. Combine all ingredients except pork chops in 3 quart shallow baking dish; mix well. Arrange chops on top, turning once to coat with sauce. Bake, uncovered, 30 to 35 minutes or until pork is no longer pink in center. Stir beans around chops once during baking. Serve with green beans or mashed potatoes, if desire. Makes 6 servings

Skillet Chicken Alfredo

Margaret Leonetti—Lutz, FL
My baby is married to Frank and they have two daughters.

1-1/4 pound chicken pieces (4-6 pieces)
1-egg, lightly beaten
½-cup Italian seasoned dry breadcrumbs
2-Tablespoons olive oil
1-jar (1 pound) Alfredo Sauce
1-small tomato, cut into 4 slices
½ cup shredded mozzarella cheese (about 2 ounces)

Dip chicken in egg, and then bread crumbs. In 12 inch nonstick skillet, heat oil over medium high heat and lightly brown chicken. Remove chicken and set aside. In that same skillet, stir in the Alfredo Sauce and bring to a boil. Reduce heat to low. Return chicken to skillet; arrange 1-tomato slice on each chicken piece. Cover and simmer 5 minutes. Now evenly top chicken with cheese and simmer, covered, an additional 2 minutes or until chicken is thoroughly cooked. Serve over hot cooked pasta and garnish with chopped fresh basil or parsley. Makes 4 servings

Basic Pancakes

David Kruger OD, Rantoul

2-cups flour (white or mixed with wheat or oat-bran flour)
3-teaspoons baking powder
1/4 cup sugar
1-teaspoon salt
2-eggs
2-cups milk
1/3 cup salad oil (or applesauce)—Hand Mix all ingredients and fry on hot griddle.

Cheeseburger Casserole

Mary Kruger, Rantoul IL

2-pounds ground beef (browned & drained)
½ cup chopped peppers
½ cup chopped onions
1 (16 ounce) can tomato sauce
½ cup ketchup
1/4 teaspoon black pepper
1-pound sliced American cheese

Brown meat and drain; add peppers and onions and fry together for a few minutes. Then add tomato sauce, ketchup, and black pepper. Stir together and cook until heated. Begin with sauce alternating layers of sauce and cheese slices in a greased casserole dish or 13x9 inch baking pan. Arrange biscuits on top of layers and Bake at 400 degrees for 20-25 minutes. Serves 10-12 (Biscuit recipe below)

Biscuits or Pizza Crust

Mary Kruger

1-cup wheat flour
½ cup oat bran flour
1-½ cup white flour
4-½ teaspoon baking powder
1-Tablespoon sugar
½ teaspoon salt
½ cup butter or margarine
1-egg
3/4 cup milk

Mix all dry ingredients together. Cut in butter till coarse and crumbly. Mix egg and milk together and stir in together quickly. Knead and pat or roll out on floured to about 1-inch for biscuits and 1/4 inch for pizza crust. Bake at 450 degrees for 12-15 minutes.

Home-made Gravy

Mary Kruger

4-Tablespoons butter
2-Tablespoons flour
2-cups broth of choice or dripping mixed with water (milk for creamy gravy)
Sausage-Optional

Melt butter in pan on medium heat; stir in flour till completely blended. Add liquid and continue to stir with wire whisk until gravy thickens; salt and pepper to taste. [What's really great is frying sausage and using that pan to make gravy with the cooked sausage and serving with biscuits. OR Use this recipe—the flour and butter with milk to make milk gravy. Then add a package dried beef or chicken cut into pieces; cook together and spread on toast. Shame on me but—my cousin would call it "Shi*! ~ on a shingle".]

Caramel Pecan Rolls

Grandma Grace Denault to Ma Connie Denault
to Mary Kruger

1-package yeast
1-cup warm water

1/4 cup sugar
1-teaspoon salt
2-Tablespoon soft margarine
1-egg
3-1/4 to 3-½ cups flour

1/3 cup margarine melted
½ cup brown sugar
1-Tablespoon clear corn syrup
2/3 cup pecan halves

4-Tablespoons melted butter (to spread on rolled out dough)

½ cup sugar and 2 teaspoon cinnamon (mixed together)

Dissolve yeast in 1-cup warm water. Stir in 1/4 cup sugar, salt, 2-Tablespoons margarine, egg, and 2 cups flour. Beat together. Work in enough of the rest of the flour to make easy to handle. Place in greased bowl and let rise in warm place that is draft free until double.

Mix together on medium burner: 1/3 cup melted margarine, ½ cup brown sugar, syrup, and pecan halves. When clear pour mixture into a greased 13x9 inch baking dish or pan.

When dough has doubled punch down, rest a few minutes, then roll out to 15x19 inches. Spread with melted butter then sprinkle with sugar, cinnamon mix. Roll up using wide side of dough. Seal edges and cut into 1-inch slices placing over nut mix in pan. Allow a little space around each roll. Cover, let rise till double and Bake at 375 degrees for 25-30 minutes; Makes about 15 rolls.

Remove from oven and let cool a minute or two. Then carefully—place a plate or dish over the top of your rolls and flip pan up-side-down. Let set like that for a few minutes so the sauce can drip down into the rolls. Remove pan. Cool just a few minutes and serve.

*　　*　　*

I don't care how poor a man is; if he has family,
he's rich. ~ Dan Wilcox and Thad Mumford,
"Identity Crisis," M*A*S*H

Cinnamon Rolls (Cinnabons)

Mary Kruger, Rantoul IL
Community Service Center Board President

2 packages yeast
1-cup warm water
1-teaspoon sugar

1-cup warm milk
2/3 cup sugar
2/3 cup melted butter
2 teaspoons salt
2-eggs (beaten)

7-8 cups flour

*Mix yeast, 1-cup warm water, and 1-teaspoon sugar in a small bowl and let set. Mix the warm milk, 2/3 cup sugar, melted butter, salt and eggs in large bowl; then add yeast mix. Add half the flour and beat till smooth. Stir in enough flour to make slightly stiff. Then turn dough onto a well floured board and knead for 5-10 minutes. *Place in well buttered glass or plastic bowl. Cover and let rise in a warm place—free from drafts—until doubled in size. *Then punch down and let rest 5 minutes. Roll out on floured surface to a 15x20 inch rectangle and spread dough with * (FILLING): ½ cup melted butter. Mix together 1-½ cup sugar with 2-teaspoons of cinnamon and sprinkle over dough. Scatter with walnut pieces and or raisons if desired. *Roll up dough and seal the ends; cut into 12-15 slices. *Coat a 13x9 inch and an 8 inch baking dish or pan with ½ cup melted butter. Sprinkle with 1/4 cup sugar then place cinnamon roll slices together in pans. *Let rise in warm place till doubled. Then Bake at 350 degrees for 25-30 minutes.

Easy-Creamy Glaze: Mix together—2/3 cup melted butter, 4 cups powdered sugar, 2 teaspoons vanilla and 4-8 Tablespoons hot water. Drizzle over warm buns. * OR—for richer thicker icing use the following frosting.

Cinnabon Frosting:

1-pound margarine
1-pound cream cheese
2-pounds powdered sugar
1-teaspoons lemon juice
2-teaspoons vanilla extract

Allow margarine and cheese to reach room temperature. Beat together in bowl with mixer slowly adding all powdered sugar. Mix for at least 12 minutes; add juice and vanilla. Ice buns while warm

Granola Snack Bars

Mary Kruger, Rantoul IL
Community Service Center Board President

½ cup butter or margarine
3/4 cup brown sugar
1/3 cup corn syrup (or honey)
1-egg
½ teaspoon vanilla
3-½ cups oats (uncooked)
1-cup chocolate chips (or whatever)

Beat margarine, sugar, and corn syrup until fluffy. Blend in the egg and vanilla. Add the oats and chocolate chips. Press batter firmly into a well greased 13x9 inch pan and Bake at 350 degrees for 20-23 minutes. Cool. Then refrigerate for an hour before cutting into 2x1-½ inch pieces. Makes 32 delicious bars

Instead of a full cup of chocolate chips you could add ½ cup with 1/4 cup raisons and 1/4 cup dried cranberries mixed with nuts. Just remember to keep your combination of ingredients to 1-cup. Otherwise your bars will not hold together. Get creative! Add marshmallows for the kids or other flavor of chips.

Caramel Corn

David Kruger OD
Rantoul, IL

2 cups brown sugar
1-cup margarine
½ cup corn syrup
1-teaspoon salt
1-teaspoon butter flavoring (optional)
½ teaspoon soda
8 quarts of popped popcorn

Combine sugar, margarine, syrup, salt and flavoring; bring to a boil. Cook 5 minutes. Remove from heat and add soda. Be ware! This will make it bubble up! That is what you want it to do! Just keep stirring until it calms down a bit then pour over popcorn and stir. Bake in large pan at 250 degrees for one hour stirring ever 15 minutes. Stir a couple times after you remove from oven so it doesn't clump together. OR—spread out on baking sheets to let dry/cool.

David says this is a great recipe when barbecuing for a crowd—and he should know. With his four children, my nine and our ten grandchildren—he's fed the multitudes.

Grilled-Chicken Rub (The meal deal using up those chicken leg quarters)

(Husband) David Kruger, OD Rantoul, IL

Chicken leg quarters can be bought in the frozen food section for about $5.00 for a ten pound bag. You'll find about twenty pieces in the bag which makes for a very economical meal. This chicken is so good, even people who only eat the white meat of a chicken will rave over it. You'll here comments like "I didn't know dark meat could taste so good!"

Rub: 4-Tablespoons paprika   [Potatoes: Wash and rinse eight to ten
         8-teaspoons salt   potatoes]
         2-teaspoons garlic powder
         2-teaspoons onion powder
         2-teaspoons black pepper

Prepare chicken: Thaw chicken. Remove as much skin from the thighs and legs as you can. (When grilling, the fatty skin makes quite a mess so you want to remove as much as you can). Combine the rub ingredients and cover chicken quarters thoroughly. Place in a covered dish or large plastic bag and let set in the refrigerator for a few hours.

Prepare grill: I prefer charcoal grills, but gas grills work fine too. Let coals get white with ash. *Wrap potatoes* in tin foil. Place on grill and close lid for ½ hour. If using sweet potatoes or other fresh vegetables, put them on the grill at the same time as the chicken. They do not need a head start. Be sure to cook with a closed lid on your grill.

Move potatoes to the side and place chicken on grill and close lid. Turn every 20 minutes and add coals as necessary to maintain good heat. Chicken should take about an hour and will take on a deep reddish color with juices running clear. The chicken will be succulent, juicy and flavorful and it's OK to eat more than one piece. (Serves 8-10 people)

Seven Layer Cookies

Mary Kruger, Rantoul IL

In a 9x13 inch cake pan melt one stick of margarine or butter in pre-heating 350 degree oven.

Then sprinkle over that:
1-cup graham cracker crumbs (distribute evenly with spoon to get a crust effect)
1-cup coconut
1-cup chocolate chips
1-cup butterscotch chips
1-can Sweetened Condensed Milk
1-cup chopped nuts of choice

Bake at 350 degrees for 30 minutes or until top starts turning golden. Cool and cut.

Chocolate Fudge Icing

Mary Kruger, Rantoul IL

3/4 cup baking cocoa
12-Tablespoons margarine or real butter (soft)
3-½ cups powdered sugar
½ cup milk
2 teaspoons vanilla extract

Beat all ingredients together until smooth. If icing is too thin add extra powdered sugar. If too thin add a few drops of water. [I always use Blue Bonnet Margarine. Cheaper margarines have a lot of water and don't work as well.] Ice your cake when it has cooled. Then spread any left over icing onto graham crackers for a delicious snack.

Vanilla Butter Icing

Mary Kruger, Rantoul IL

1/3 cup soft margarine or butter
3-cups powdered sugar
1-½ teaspoons vanilla
2-Tablespoons milk

Mix together until smooth. Once again I always use Blue Bonnet margarine for the best results. To make colored icing just add the food coloring of your choice and mix well.

Peach Cobbler

Mary Kruger, Rantoul IL
Handed down from my mother Connie Denault

2 (1-pound, 13-ounce) cans sliced peaches with juice
1-½ teaspoon cinnamon
5-Tablespoons cornstarch

Cook till thickens and boils. Stir constantly. Keep hot.

3-cups flour
3-Tablespoons sugar
4-½ teaspoons baking powder
1-½ teaspoon salt
8-Tablespoons shortening
1-½ cup milk

Mix till dough forms balls. Drop by teaspoonfuls onto hot peach filling. Bake at 400 degrees in a 3-quart casserole dish for 30 minutes.

Community Service Center of Northern Champaign County

A Story of Hope

The Community Service Center of Northern Champaign County is a not-for-profit organization that has been providing mental health, social health and welfare services to residents of Northern Champaign County since 1971.

The First Call for Help program provides information and referrals to human services including an emergency food pantry, case management, prescription assistance, clothing center referrals, the holiday bureau, as well as transportation to special medical, mental health, social and welfare agencies that are not available in Rantoul.

In the 2007 fiscal year (June '06-June '07) 4,126 individuals received food assistance, 82 were helped with baby needs, 507 received help with transportation, 99 gas vouchers were issued, 10 residents were assisted with utilities, 321 received holiday assistance, 30 individuals received help with prescriptions, 202 were given clothing referrals and 42 received case management.

The most recent addition to the CSC is its Eye Glass Distribution Services. Individuals or families with a Medicaid/Medical Card and a recent prescription for eye glasses are now able order their frames at the Community Service Center on Tuesday afternoons from 1:00-4:00 p.m. Minor repairs and adjustments to frames can also be made during those times.

The agency's Rantoul Area Project (RAP) is a grassroots effort, established in 1987 allowing residents to organize, develop and carry out a plan to improve conditions that put youth at risk. The RAP works year round to strengthen at-risk neighborhoods by coordinating committees of local volunteers to provide programs and activities aimed at reducing and preventing juvenile delinquency. Some of the activities include nutrition classes, tutoring, after school programs, holiday parties, field trips, teen events, advocacy and referral.

The Kid's Foundation was established in 1992 by Bob Kidd. A sort of hero to needy children Kidd noticed there were some local children who couldn't afford to participate in recreation programs so he decided to make a difference. Although the Rantoul Township High School teacher-coach passed away in 1994 his program lives on. Economically disadvantaged youth from kindergarten through eighth grade who live in the Rantoul, Thomasboro, Ludlow, Flatville and Gifford areas can apply through the CSC. Eligibility is determined by the CSC, representatives of the Recreation Department, the park district and the Kid's Foundation Executive Board. For more information on how you can help contact Treasurer Michael Fox at 892-2143 or President Al Vogelsang at 893-1185.

The Holiday Bureau program provides food baskets as well as toys to low income families at Christmas time. Local businesses and community members donate a wide variety of food items as well as new toys and games for parents or guardians of needy children to choose from.

The Supportive Services for agencies located outside Rantoul using the Community Service Center as a satellite site to bring services to area residents includes the use of office space, telephone, copier, reception service and consultation.

There are 18 different agencies utilizing the CSC facilities to have 2,358 contacts with clients. Of the agencies or programs with regularly scheduled hours at the CSC are the Mental Health Center, East Central Illinois Refugee and Mutual Assistance Center, Prairie Center Health Systems, the Illinois Migrant Council, Champaign County Regional Planning Commission, Extension Service's Family Nutrition Program, LIHEAP Energy Assistance Program, A Woman's Fund Rape Crisis Service, and Kruger Vision. Other human service agencies also schedule appointments at the Center as needed.

There is no fee charged for services provided by the Community Service Center. However, some agencies working out of the facility do charge according to a sliding fee schedule based on client's financial capabilities.

The agency serves the nine townships of northern Champaign County including Brown, Compromise, Condit, East Bend, Harwood, Kerr, Ludlow, Newcomb, and Rantoul. The staff of the CSC keeps all information confidential.

The CSC is governed by an 11 member Board of Directors each representing different professions and Townships of Northern Champaign County. Funding is provided by the Champaign County Mental Health Board, United Way of Champaign County, the Dept. of Human Services, the Villages of Rantoul, Gifford and Thomasboro, the Townships of Ludlow and Compromise as well as private donations from organizations and individuals. Additional support is provided by over 40 volunteers.

For more information on these services or to offer your assistance call the Community Service Center at 217-893-1530 between 8:30 a.m. and 5:00 p.m. Monday through Friday, or visit their office at 520 E. Wabash Avenue, Suite 1, Rantoul. You may leave a message after hours. For mental health emergencies call the Crisis Line at 217-359-4141.

* * *

Sharon Thompson has been the Secretary/Bookkeeper for the Community Service Center for 8 years. As board president I told her I wasn't going to let her retire—but somehow I don't think that carried much weight. She's been a true asset to our staff.

Corn Casserole

Sharon Thompson
Community Service Center, Secretary/Bookkeeper

1-Box Jiffy Corn Bread Mix
1-Can Whole Kernel Corn (drained)
1-Can Creamed Corn
1-Stick Butter (Melted)
8 ounces sour cream

Mix together and bake at 350 degrees for 40 minutes or until done.

Andy Kulczycki has served as Executive Director for the Community Service Center of Northern Champaign County for 19 years now. His incredible management skills and concern for the communities of northern Champaign County has brought the CSC through some very challenging times; especially since the closing of Chanute Air Force Base 1993. Andy's many years of hard work and dedication continues to bless our neighborhoods.

Andy's Mexican Casser(ole')

Andy Kulczycki, Urbana IL
Executive Director Community Service Center in Rantoul IL

1-pound lean hamburger
½ green pepper, chopped
1-small onion, chopped
2-cloves garlic, sliced very thin
2-stalks celery, chopped
2-cups cooked rice
1-(12 ounce) can enchilada sauce
1-(12 ounce) can tomato sauce
1-(4 ounce) can chopped chilies
1½ cups shredded cheddar cheese
1-can black olives, sliced

Cook the rice (regular or minute rice will work fine). Next, brown the hamburger in a large pan and drain the fat. Add pepper, onion, garlic, and celery; sauté until onions turn translucent. Add enchilada sauce, tomato sauce, chili peppers, and olives. Stir and let bubble gently on medium heat for about 5-minutes. "Watch it," Andy says "the stuff can splatter."

Put the cooked rice in a large casserole dish. Add the mixture from the pan and most of the cheese. Mix well. Spread the remaining cheese on top of the casserole. Cook in 350 degree oven for 20-minutes or on high in a microwave for 5-½ minutes. Total prep and cooking time is less than and hour "if you can chop those veggies fast." (Serves 6) As far as calories per serving—Andy says "Forget about it!" Just enjoy it! He says "A hearty red wine or an amber ale go well with this dish."

Chili Dip

Betty McKaufsky—Rantoul, Illinois
Previous CSC Board Member

1-pound ground beef
1-green pepper chopped fine
1 (1-3/4 ounce) envelope chili seasoning
1-6 ounce can tomato paste
1-3 ounce package cream cheese
1-cup water

Cook ground beef and green peppers in skillet stirring to crumble until beef is brown. Drain off excess fat. Stir in chili mix, tomato paste, cream cheese and water. Cook over medium heat until it comes to a boil. Pour in fondue pot or crock-pot and dip with corn chips.

Cheddar Biscuits

Crystal Hennigh—Rantoul, Illinois

1-cup Bisquick
1/3 cup milk
½ cup cheddar cheese
1/4 teaspoon garlic powder
1/4 teaspoon parsley flakes

Mix Bisquick, milk, cheese, garlic powder and parsley flakes together and drop in six pieces onto an un-greased cookie sheet. Bake at 450 degrees for 8-10 minutes. Watch not to over bake. Brush with topping (1/4 cup melted butter and 1/4 teaspoon garlic powder) while warm.

Chocolate Cherry Cookies

Marilyn L. Dewey
Founding Executive Director for CSC, Rantoul, IL

½ cup butter
1-cup sugar
1-large egg
3/4 cup soured milk
1-teaspoon vanilla extract
1-3/4 cup all purpose flour
½ teaspoon baking soda
½ teaspoon salt
½ cup cocoa, unsweetened powder (baking cocoa)
2-cups dried tart cherries

Mix butter, sugar and egg thoroughly. Stir in sour milk, (made by adding 3/4 Tablespoon lemon juice to enough milk to measure 3/4 cup and let stand 1-hour at room temperature) and vanilla. Sift flour, salt, baking soda, and cocoa together and blend in. Add cherries and mix well. Drop by rounded teaspoonful about 2 inches apart on a lightly greased cookie sheet. Bake at 375 degrees for 8-10 minutes. Allow to stand one minute before removing from cookie sheet.

Meat Loaf Pie

Marilyn L. Dewey
Founding Executive Director for CSC, Rantoul, IL

½ cup sliced celery (and chopped onion to taste)
1-Tablespoon vegetable oil
1-pound ground beef
1-package Jif Corn Muffin Mix

Sauté celery and onion in oil for about 5 minutes; add beef and brown. Drain fat and blend in 6 ounces evaporated milk (a small can). Add salt and pepper to taste. Heat, but do not boil. Place in 1-½ quart baking dish. Prepare 1-package of Jif corn muffin mix according to package directions and spoon over meat mixture—making sure to cover the meat and seal the edges with muffin mix. Bake at 400 degrees for 25 minutes and serve.

One of Elsie's early Community Service Center memories was when Marilyn Derby came up to her, as they were removing their choir robes on a Sunday morning, explaining that a new agency was being formed in Rantoul to "help people." Marilyn went on to say that she thought Elsie would be an asset and would enjoy the type of work it involved. Having not worked for ten years Elsie had to give it some thought and discuss it with her husband. Since it was only part time she decided to take the job. She remembered how small their budget expenses were. All they had was their salaries and the telephone bill. At that time The Methodist church donated the use of one room and one of the staff members brought a card table, note paper and ink pens. "That was it" she said. Then after several years of seeing that the agency was a success Elsie took numerous sociology courses offered by the University of Illinois on the Chanute Air Force Base. She worked a total of 22 years for the CSC and for "every director" as she puts it. Elsie enjoyed seeing what "imprint each would leave on the agency and in what direction they would lead."

Corn Pudding

Elsie Womer, CSC Case Aide for 22 years—Rantoul, IL

1-can creamed corn
1-egg
1-Tablespoon sugar
1/3 cup cream or evaporated milk
1-Tablespoon flour
Salt & Pepper to taste
Butter or substitute

Beat egg; add creamed corn and sugar. Place cream or milk and flour in small bowl and mix well with whisk. Add to corn mixture. Grease an 8x8 inch casserole dish or pan with butter or substitute and pour in corn mixture. Place 2-3 small pats of butter or substitute on top. Bake at 350 degrees for 1-hour—or until nicely browned. Ingredients may be added to make larger amounts. (1-egg per can) Elsie notes that when she makes this for a potluck dinner she uses 5-6 cans of corn plus the other ingredients—using no more than 3 Tablespoons of sugar—and it fills a 9x13 inch baking dish. Her family likes this baked long enough that even the sides are crispy.

Dutch Cookie

Sharon Thompson
Community Service Center
Secretary

1-cup butter or margarine
1-cup sugar
1-egg separateds
2 cups flour
½ teaspoon cinnamon
1-teaspoon water

Mix butter, sugar and egg yolk. Measure flour by dipping method or sifting; blend flour and cinnamon then stir into butter mixture. Pat into greased cookie sheet. Beat water and egg white until frothy then brush over dough. Sprinkle with nuts. Bake at 350 degrees for 20-25 minutes; or until lightly browned then cut immediately into finger like strips. Makes 50—1x3 inch cookies

Easy Sugar Buns

Crystal Hennigh—Rantoul Illinois

2-cups biscuit mix
2-Tablespoons sugar
1-teaspoon nutmeg
1/8 teaspoon cinnamon
2/3 cup cream
1-½ cups milk
1-egg

Pre-heat oven to 400 degrees; mix biscuit mix, sugar, nutmeg and cinnamon together then add the cream, milk and egg. Mix thoroughly and drop dough into greased muffin cups filling cups ½ full. Bake about 15 minutes. Let sit 5-10 minutes then dip warm buns into 1/4 cup melted butter, then ½ cup sugar—coating all. Serve warm. Yields 10-12 buns

---

Karen Kelly has worked with the Community Service Center for 21 years. She exemplifies the words of Benjamin Franklin, *"No one is useless in this world who lightens the burden of it for someone else."* Karen is one of the most caring, non-judgmental people I have ever met. It has been a true blessing to not only have been able to work with her but to have her serving our clients at the CSC.

Ginni's Chiles Rellenos

Karen Kelly
CSC Service Coordinator, Rantoul IL

1/4 cup butter or margarine
1-7 ounce can diced green chilies, drained
½ pound cheddar cheese, shredded
½ pound Monterey Jack cheese, shredded
3-eggs
2-cups milk
3/4 teaspoon salt
1-cup biscuit mix

Melt butter in 13x9 inch baking dish. Arrange chilies in a layer in bottom of dish. Cover with cheeses. Blend the eggs, milk, salt and biscuit mix in a mixing bowl. Pour over cheese in baking dish. Bake at 350 degrees until golden, 40 minutes (or more). Let cool slightly and cut into squares. Serve with salsa and/or hot sauce.

Cocoa Syrup

Brian Truncale, Rantoul, IL
Volunteer for CSC Food Pantry

1-cup baking cocoa (and a pinch of salt)
1-1/4 cup sugar
1-1/4 cup water

Mix all ingredients together then bring to boil over low heat. Simmer 5 minutes, stirring constantly. Cool. Add 1-teaspoon vanilla.

Grandma Briggs Molasses Cookies

Karen Kelly
CSC Office Coordinator, Rantoul IL

1-cup brown sugar
1-cup white sugar
1-cup margarine
2-eggs
½ cup dark molasses (or sorghum)
4 cups flour
2 teaspoon cinnamon
2 teaspoon ginger
2-½ teaspoons baking soda
½ teaspoon salt
Cinnamon & sugar

Cream together the sugars and margarine. Blend the eggs and molasses into the creamed ingredients. Mix in the dry ingredients (except for the "cinnamon & sugar"). Chill overnight. Form into 1-inch balls and roll in cinnamon and sugar mix. Bake on greased cookie sheet for 8-minutes at 375 degrees.

Meat Loaf Vegetable Casserole

Marilyn L. Dewey
Founding Executive Director for CSC, Rantoul, IL

1-½ pound lean ground beef
3/4 cup bread crumbs
8 ounces tomato sauce
2 Tablespoons water
1-teaspoon prepared mustard
1-teaspoon salt
1-Tablespoon dried minced onion
1/4 teaspoon pepper

Mix together all above and set aside. Spray a 2 quart casserole dish with cooking oil and put the following into the dish:

1-32 ounce package frozen mixed vegetables
2-sliced potatoes
1-sliced onion
1-teaspoon salt

Put meat mix on top of veggies making sure to cover everything completely. Bake at 350 degrees for 1-1/4 hours.

Mexican Salad

Betty McKaufsky—Rantoul, IL
Previous CSC Board Member

1-pound hamburger cooked & drained
Add 15 ounce can kidney beans & simmer 10 minutes. Let cool.

Toss with the following:

1-head lettuce diced
2-medium tomatoes diced
1-onion chopped fine
4-ounces grated cheddar cheese
8-ounce bottle French dressing (Use as much or as little as you'd like)
8 ounces Taco Sauce

Serve with tortilla chips.

Ola's Fudge Nut Bars

Karen Kelly
CSC Office Coordinator, Rantoul IL

1-cup margarine
2 cups brown sugar
2 eggs
2 teaspoons vanilla
2-½ cups flour
1-teaspoon soda
1-teaspoon salt
3 cups oatmeal
1-12 ounce package chocolate chips
1-can condensed milk
2 Tablespoons margarine
½ teaspoon salt
1-cup nuts
2-teaspoons vanilla

Cream 1-cup margarine and sugar; add eggs and vanilla. Sift flour, soda, salt and stir in oatmeal. Add to creamed mixture. Set aside. Melt together chocolate chips, milk, 2-Tablespoons margarine and salt. Stir in nuts and vanilla. Spread two thirds of the batter into a 10x15 inch pan. Cover with chocolate chip mixture. Drop remaining batter over filling.

Bake 15-20 minutes at 350 degrees.

Peanut Butter Bread

Brian Truncale, Rantoul, IL
Volunteer for CSC Food Pantry

1-½ cups flour
1-cup sugar
1-Tablespoon baking powder
½ teaspoon salt
½ cup peanut butter
1-cup rolled oats
1-egg
1-cup milk
(*Optional—½ teaspoon cinnamon)

Sift flour, sugar, baking powder and salt together in a bowl. Cut in peanut butter until mixture resembles coarse crumbs. Add oats, egg and milk stirring only until blended. Pour into loaf pan. Bake at 350 degrees for 1-hour. Done when toothpick comes out dry.

Peanut Butter Cookies—(No Flour)

Sharon Thompson
Community Service Center—Secretary/Bookkeeper

1-cup peanut butter
1-cup sugar
1-egg
½ teaspoon vanilla

Mix peanut butter and sugar. Add remaining ingredients. Shape into 1-inch balls and put on un-greased cookie sheet. Press with fort to flatten slightly.

Bake at 350 degrees for 12-15 minutes. Makes 3 dozen.

When doubling this recipe use 18 ounce jar of peanut butter. (That equals 2 cups).

Quick Cottage Cheese Salad

Sharon Thompson
Community Service Center—Secretary/Bookkeeper

1 (16 ounce) Trim & lite (low-fat) cottage cheese
1 (3 ounce) sugar-free orange Jell-o
1 (8 ounce) container lite Cool Whip
1 (20 ounce) can crushed pineapple, drained
1 small can mandarin oranges, drained

Sprinkle jell-o over cottage cheese; mix well. Add pineapple and oranges. Fold in Cool Whip.

YUM-A-SETTA

Sharon Thompson
Community Service Center—Secretary/Bookkeeper

2 pounds hamburger
Salt and pepper to taste
Little brown sugar
1/4 onion, chopped
1-can tomato soup, undiluted
1-can cream of chicken soup, undiluted
1-package (16 ounces) egg noodles
1-package (8 ounces) processed cheese

Brown hamburger with salt, pepper, brown sugar and onion then add tomato soup. Cook egg noodles and drain. Add cream of chicken soup. Layer hamburger mixture and noodle mixture in casserole dish with processed cheese between layers.

Bake at 350 degrees for ½ hour.

Zucchini Quiche

Linda Hennigh—Rantoul, Illinois

1/4 cup oil
2 cup grated zucchini
1-medium chopped onion
1-cup shredded cheese
3 eggs
1-cup Bisquick
Salt and pepper

Mix zucchini, onion, cheese, oil, and eggs together then add the Bisquick and mix well. Pour into greased pie dish, sprinkle salt and pepper. Bake at 350 degrees for 45 minutes.

French Toast

Mary Kruger—passed down from her mother Connie Denault

5-Eggs
1/4 cup milk
1-teaspoon vanilla extract
1/4 cup sugar
10-12 slices bread of your choice

Mix ingredients well. Dip both sides of the bread into mixture and fry on buttered grill. Flip over as sides become golden or cooked to your liking. Raison bread works great. (A good point to remember when making French toast from scratch is that fresh bread will be too soft and difficult to work with. So this recipe is a great way to use up stale or day old bread.) Store left over French toast in the refrigerator and warm up in toaster or microwave. [My kids love peanut butter and syrup on their French toast. Raisin Bread also makes a delicious French toast!]

Churches

Our community churches are to be commended for their continued tireless efforts in keeping the food pantry shelves stocked at the Community Service Center. These are without fail some of the most generous and giving people around. Not to mention—how great of cooks they are as well. The world is truly a better place because of our church friends! ~ Thank you for all for your wonderful support! We appreciate what you do!

This ***Houska*** recipe came from Prague, Czechoslovakia. Pauline Klapka Flick's great grandfather, her grand parents and her father all came over to the United States in 1901. They were stow-a-ways, living in the bottom of the ship with some other Bohemians. They landed at Ellis Island. Pauline's father told his six children that when he saw the Statue of Liberty he knew he was free. "His stories of the old country were very interesting," Pauline said. This braided bread was prepared at Christmas time in Czechoslovakia. "However" Pauline says, "over here we make any time of the year. It is sweet bread that we eat with coffee—much like coffee and donuts here. It's very good warm with butter."

Houska (Bohemian Christmas Bread)

Pauline (Klapka) Flick—Rantoul Christian Church

1/4 cup lukewarm milk (115-120 degrees)
1-package active dry yeast
1-teaspoon sugar
4 3/4-5 cups flour
½ cup sugar
1-teaspoon salt
1-teaspoon grated lemon rind
Pinch of nutmeg

1-cup luke warm milk
2-whole eggs plus 1-yolk
½ cup butter softened
½ cup slivered almonds
½ cup white raisins
1-Tablespoon water

Dissolve yeast in warm milk. Stir in 1-teaspoon sugar. Set in a warm place until mixture has doubled in volume (about 10 minutes). Combine 4-½ cups flour, the sugar, salt, lemon peel and nutmeg in large mixing bowl. Add yeast mixture, milk, eggs, and butter. Beat until a medium stiff dough forms. Turn out onto a lightly floured surface. Knead in enough remaining flour to form stiff dough. Continue kneading until dough is smooth and satiny (about 10 minutes). Place in buttered bowl turning to butter top of dough. Cover and let rise in a warm place until double in bulk (about 1-hour). Punch dough down and knead in nuts and raisins. Divide dough in half' cut each half into 5 pieces. Roll each piece on lightly floured surface to form a rope 12 inches by 1-inch. On a greased cookie sheet, braid three of the ropes tucking under the ends. Then twist the remaining two ropes and place on top of braid. Repeat with remaining half of dough. Cover and let rise in warm place until double in bulk (about 45 minutes). Combine egg white and water. Carefully brush top of braids with mixture. Bake 30-35 minutes or until golden in a 350 degree oven. Remove from baking sheets.

Chicken Casserole

Joan Winfrey
Crossroad of Life Community Church

2-cups chopped cooked chicken
½ cup chopped pecans
2-teaspoons dried minced onions
1-cup sliced celery
1-cup mayonnaise
2-teaspoons lemon juice
1-cup potato chips broken
½ cup shredded cheese

Mix first six ingredients together. Place in a greased 1-½ quart casserole dish. Mix broken potato chips and cheese then sprinkle on top. Bake uncovered at 375 degrees for 30 minutes or until heated. Yields 6 servings

Sweet Potato Casserole (Using Fresh Potatoes)

Joan Winfrey

4 cups sweet potatoes cooked, peeled, and mashed
1/3 cup butter melted
2 eggs beaten
½ cup carnation evaporated milk
2 teaspoons vanilla extract
½ cup sugar

Topping: ½ cup chopped nuts, ½ cup packed brown sugar, 3 Tablespoons butter melted

In large bowl, combine mashed potatoes, butter, eggs, milk, vanilla and sugar. Spread into a 1-½ quart casserole dish. Combine all topping ingredients and sprinkle over potatoes. Bake at 375 degrees for 25 minutes. Yield 6-8 servings

Au Gratin Potatoes

Sue Ludwig
First Assembly of God Church, Rantoul IL

12 baked potatoes (not fully cooked)—sliced
Stick of butter
1-can cream of chicken soup
Velveeta sliced
Salt and pepper

Layer half the potatoes in large pan or casserole dish. Dot with butter then spread cream of chicken soup over potatoes. Salt and pepper to season. Layer slices of Velveeta cheese over soup; repeat layers. Bake at 350 degrees for 30 minutes.

Apple Crisp

Sue Ludwig
First Assembly of God Church, Rantoul IL

8 cups apples—peeled and sliced
1-teaspoon cinnamon
1-teaspoon salt
1/4 cup water
3/4 cup flour
1-cup sugar
1/3 cup soft margarine

Place sliced apples into a 13x9 inch baking dish. Mix cinnamon, salt, and water and sprinkle over apples. Rub flour, sugar and margarine together until crumbly and sprinkle over apples. Bake at 350 degrees for 40 minutes. Serve warm with ice cream or cool whip.

Apple Pie Bars

Sharon Ingold
First Assembly of God Church

1-recipe pie dough
2 cups applesauce (chunky)
1-½ teaspoons cinnamon
2/3 cup flour
2/3 cup sugar
½ stick margarine softened
2/3 cup raisins (optional)

Roll out pie dough and put on cookie sheet. Mix applesauce, raisins and 1-teaspoon cinnamon. Spread over dough. Stir together flour, sugar and ½ teaspoon cinnamon and margarine until crumbly. Sprinkle over applesauce mixture. Bake at 350 degrees for about 40 minutes or until light brown. Cut into bars.

Avocado Dip

Sue Ludwig
First Assembly of God Church, Rantoul IL

1-ripe avocado, mashed
½ cup mayonnaise
½ cup sour cream
2-Tablespoon buttermilk
3-teaspoons white vinegar
1/4 teaspoon salt
1/4 teaspoon parsley
1/4 teaspoon dill weed
1/4 teaspoon garlic powder
1/4 teaspoon pepper

Mix well, chill and serve with chips or vegetables.

Better-Than-Anything Cake

Janice Kizer
First Assembly of God Church, Rantoul IL

1-box German chocolate cake mix
1-can (14 ounce) sweetened condensed milk (Eagle brand)
1-jar (16 ounce) caramel or butterscotch topping
1-(8 ounce) frozen whipped topping, thawed
1-cup toffee chips

Bake cake according to box instructions. Heat oven to cake mix package directions and bake the cake. Cool 15 minutes; then poke holes in top of warm cake with handle of wooden spoon. Drizzle the sweetened condensed milk evenly over cake; then drizzle topping over that. Cover and refrigerate for 2-hours. Spread with whipped topping and sprinkle toffee chips. Store covered in refrigerator. Serves 15

Bisquick Turkey Pot Pie

Janice Kizer
First Assembly of God Church, Rantoul IL

1-can cream of chicken soup
1-cup chopped turkey
1-bag frozen vegetables
1-1/4 cups Bisquick
½ cup milk
1-egg

Preheat oven to 400 degrees. Combine soup, turkey and vegetables in 9-inch pie plate. Stir remaining ingredients, pour over turkey mixture and bake 30 minutes.

Broccoli Casserole

Sharon Ingold
First Assembly of God Church, Rantoul IL

1-cup Minute Rice, uncooked
3/4 cup chopped onion
3/4 cup chopped celery
1-stick melted margarine
1-can cream of mushroom soup
1-can cream of chicken soup
1-box chopped broccoli, thawed
1-small jar Cheez Whiz
Salt and pepper

Melt butter and add with other ingredients except Cheez Whiz. Put in casserole dish and put Cheez Whiz on top by spoonfuls.

Bake covered 45 minutes at 350 degrees.

Broccoli Salad

Sharon Ingold
First Assembly of God Church, Rantoul IL

1-bunch raw broccoli, chopped
1-can mushrooms, drained
1-can water chestnuts, drained and chopped
1 (8 ounce) package Kraft Zesty Italian dressing

Marinate overnight and turn several times.

Chicken Soup

Sharon Ingold
First Assembly of God Church, Rantoul IL

1-whole chicken
1-onion
Carrots
Celery
Egg noodles, thin
Salt and pepper

Cook chicken in pot of water on stove until tender. Save stock. Remove chicken from bone. Dice up onion, celery and carrots and cook in broth. Add noodles, salt, pepper, and any other spices desired. Add chicken pieces. Simmer a few minutes and serve.

Chicks Potatoes

Sharon Ingold
First Assembly of God Church, Rantoul IL

8 potatoes
1-stick margarine
1-small container sour cream
3 Tablespoons Lawrey's seasoned salt

Boil potatoes with jackets. Cool, peel and dice. Place in baking dish. Melt margarine, sour cream and seasoning salt together. Pour over potatoes and bake at 350 degrees for ½ hour.

Egg Custard Pie

Sharon Ingold
First Assembly of God Church

6 eggs
1-½ cups sugar
2 cups milk
1-teaspoon nutmeg

Beat eggs well then add sugar, milk and nutmeg. Put into a 10-inch unbaked pie shell and bake at 350 degrees until brown or jelly like.

Creamy Italian Chicken

Janice Kizer
First Assembly of God Church, Rantoul

4 boneless skinless chicken breast halves
1-envelope Italian salad dressing
1/4 cup water
1-(8 ounce) cream cheese, softened
1-(10-3/4 ounce) can cream of chicken soup
1-(4 ounce) can mushroom stems & pieces, drained
Hot cooked rice or noodles

Place chicken in slow cooker. Combine salad dressing and water then pour over chicken. Cover and cook on low for 3 hours. In a small bowl beat cream cheese and soup, stir in mushrooms. Pour over chicken and cook another hour or until chicken juices run clear. Serve over rice or noodles. Yield 4 servings.

Creamy Rice Pudding

Sharon Ingold
First Assembly of God Church, Rantoul IL

½ cup uncooked rice
3 cups boiling water
1-½ teaspoon salt
1-can Eagle Brand milk
1/4 teaspoon nutmeg
½ cup seedless raisins (optional)
2-eggs
1-teaspoon vanilla extract

Cook together on low heat until thick. Stir often.

Salami

Sharon Ingold
First Assembly of God Church, Rantoul IL

2 pounds lean ground beef
1-cup water
½ teaspoon garlic powder
½ teaspoon onion powder
2 Tablespoons Morton's Tender Quick salt
1-Tablespoon cracked black peppercorns
Dash of red pepper

Mix well and form into 2 rolls. Wrap in foil and refrigerator for 24 hours. Prick bottom of foil (to let drippings out). Place on rack in pan and bake for 1-½ hours at 350 degrees. Cool in foil and store in refrigerator or freezer.

Egg Roll

Aggie Bagtas—Rantoul, IL
First Assembly of God Church

2-pounds ground beef
½ cup ball onion finely chopped
½ cup green onion finely chopped
½ cup carrot finely chopped
½ cup celery finely chopped
½ water chestnut chopped
1/4 teaspoon salt
½ teaspoon ground pepper
½ teaspoon garlic salt
1-Box Lumpia Wrapper (peel separately and cut in halves)

Simmer beef until juice is produced and almost brown. Drain the meat putting the juice in a small container to "froze" in the refrigerator. Throw away the frozen fat and put the juice back in the meat. Combine all the above ingredients in a bowl adding two eggs and cornstarch. Mix thoroughly and spoon a full teaspoon on a half wrapper. Roll tightly to the end, brush with water to seal. Deep fry in a low temperature heat until golden brown to serve.

Fried Chicken Tenders

Elaine Cler
First Assembly of God Church, Rantoul IL

1-package Tyson chicken tenders
1-cup of flour
2/3 cup of oil
3-eggs
1/4 cup of milk

Beat eggs in a bowl and stir in milk. Place flour in good size bowl. Put oil in frying pan and get good and hot. Dip tenders in egg and milk mixture, then dip in flour and place in skillet. Fry both sides to a golden brown, sprinkling salt and pepper on both sides. Turn temperature on burner to low and cook for one hour with lid on and not turning. Remove from skillet on to plate and let set for 10 minutes.

Pie Crust

Sharon Ingold
First Assembly of God Church

3 cups flour
1-cup shortening or lard
1-egg, beaten
1-Tablespoon vinegar
6 Tablespoons water
Dash of salt

Mix water, vinegar, lard, egg, salt and beat with fork. Work in flour.

Hash Brown Potato Casserole

Janice Kizer
First Assembly of God Church, Rantoul

2 pounds frozen hash brown potatoes—thawed
½ cup margarine, softened
1-teaspoon salt
1/4 teaspoon pepper
1-cup chopped onion
1-can cream of chicken soup
2 cups grated cheese
16 ounces sour cream
2 cups crushed corn flakes
1/4 cup margarine

Mix first six ingredients and add grated cheese. Fold in sour cream. Melt the 1/4 cup margarine and stir in crushed corn flakes. Sprinkle on casserole. Bake in 13x9 inch dish at 350 degrees for 45-60 minutes.

Italian Beef

Sue Ludwig
First Assembly of God Church, Rantoul IL

3-5 pound beef roast
1-teaspoon oregano
1-teaspoon basil
2-teaspoons garlic powder
1-teaspoon crushed red pepper
1-Tablespoon salt
1-2 bay leaves
2 cups hot water

Mix spices with hot water and pour over roast in crock-pot. Cook for 10 hours. When tender shred meat and allow meat to simmer in juice

J.J.'s Chicken Salad

J.J. Coffin
First Assembly of God Church, Rantoul IL

Chicken
Hard-boiled eggs
Sweet pickle relish
Miracle Whip
Red seedless grapes
Celery
Chopped pecans
Mustard
Garlic powder, Onion powder, Paprika & Celery salt

Cook and cut up chicken and eggs. Chop celery. Cut grapes in half then mix all ingredients together and season to taste.—This is one of those recipes where the quantity of each item is up to your taste discretion.

Lemon Cookies

Janice Kizer
First Assembly of God Church, Rantoul IL

1-cup flour
½ cup melted margarine or butter
1/4 cup powdered sugar

Mix flour, butter, sugar then press in greased 8x8 inch cake pan. Bake 20 minutes at 325 degrees.

2 eggs, beaten
1-cup sugar
Pinch of salt
4 Tablespoons lemon juice

Mix and pour over crust and bake again; this time for 30 minutes at 325. Sprinkle with 2 Tablespoons powdered sugar. While warm, cut and remove from pan to cool.

Oatmeal Bars

Sharon Ingold
First Assembly of God Church

1-cup brown sugar
½ cup white sugar
4 cups oatmeal
1-cup shortening or 2 sticks soft margarine

Frosting: 1-cup chocolate chips and ½ cup peanut butter

Mix ingredients and press into greased cookie sheet. Bake at 375 degrees for 5-10 minutes. When cool melt chocolate chips and peanut butter in double boiler (or microwave). Then frost and refrigerate.

Old Time Cocoa Fudge

Elaine Cler
First Assembly of God Church, Rantoul IL

3 cups sugar
2/3 cup of Hershey cocoa
1/8 teaspoon salt
1-½ cup milk
1/4 cup butter
1-teaspoon vanilla

Butter a 9-inch square pan. In a heavy 4-quart saucepan, combine sugar, cocoa and salt. Stir in milk. Cook over medium heat stirring constantly until mixture comes to a full boil. Boil without stirring until softball stage. Drop a bit into cup of cold water to see if it forms a soft ball. Remove from heat; add butter and vanilla. Beat until fudge thickens and looses most of its gloss. Quickly pour into greased pan and cool in refrigerator. Cut into squares when fudge is set.

Peanut Brittle

Mary Saunders, First Assembly of God Church, Rantoul IL
Mary received this recipe several years ago from Alice Slade of Champaign, IL
and says it brings great joy to her heart each time she brings it out

3-cups sugar
1-cup white syrup
1-cup water
2-cups raw peanuts
2-Tablespoons Imperial margarine
1-teaspoon pure vanilla
2-Tablespoons baking soda
1/4-teaspoon salt

Bring sugar, syrup and water (stirring occasionally) to 250 degrees on a candy thermometer. Add peanuts stirring to prevent nuts from burning—to 310 degrees on candy thermometer. Remove from heat; add margarine and vanilla (stirring thoroughly until margarine melts and vanilla is stirred well into mixture.) Add baking soda and salt stirring until mixture begins to foam high (be sure soda is mixed well in mixture). Pour on to a well buttered surface. PULL WHILE HOT! Be careful while handling. Really makes a bad burn. Yields 2-½ pounds of candy

Mary says the ideal surface would be a porcelain tabletop. If regular table is used, she recommends placing a pad on the table—such as a blanket—then cover that with aluminum foil and a heavy clear plastic like Visqueen. Place two flat cookie sheets upside down on padded surface then pour half the mixture on each pan and proceed to pull while hot.

Pepperoni Bread

Sandy Heiser and Mary Saunders
First Assembly of God Church, Rantoul IL

One loaf of frozen bread dough cut in half and thawed.
Provolone cheese (Have deli slice cheese & place paper between slices)
Pepperoni (Large from deli and sliced)

After bread is thawed—do not let it set or rise—roll out long thing and wide enough pieces to accommodate cheese with enough lap on each side to wrap (fold over).

Place rolled out dough on long bread pan or cookie sheet, layer cheese, then layer pepperoni using about ½-pound of the sliced cheese (approx. 7 slices) and ½-pound of the pepperoni (about 12-14 slices) per half a loaf of bread. Wrap extra dough over meat and cheese bringing up the ends to seal. Pinch so bread does not come open in the oven.

Bake 15 minutes at 400 degrees. Serve with salad and a dessert. Serves 3-4 people

Pickled Carrots

Sharon Ingold
First Assembly of God Church, Rantoul IL

2 pound carrots, peeled and sliced
2 green peppers, sliced round
2 onions, sliced
Salt and pepper

Sauce:
1-can tomato soup
½ cup salad oil
1-cup sugar
½ cup vinegar

Cook carrots till barely tender. Layer peppers and onions in glass bowl; then sprinkle with salt and pepper. Mix sauce and pour over veggies. Let sit overnight

Raisin Coconut Pie

Sharon Ingold
First Assembly of God Church, Rantoul IL

½ box raisins
3 egg yolks
3/4 cup coconut
2 big Tablespoons flour
½ teaspoon nutmeg
½ teaspoon cinnamon
1-cup sugar
1-cup milk
2 teaspoons vanilla

Meringue: 3 egg whites and 3/4 cup sugar

Cook raisins in water to cover—until tender. Drain off most of the water. Mix rest of ingredients and add to raisins cooking on low heat until thick. Put into a baked pie shell and cover with meringue. Bake at 350 degrees until brown.

Ice Cream Dessert

Pam Adamet
St. Malachy Church, Rantoul

2 packages of ice cream sandwiches (24 count)
Place one layer of sandwiches in a 9x13 pan.
Cover with a small layer of cool whip.
Drizzle fudge ice cream topping over the cool whip and top with crushed peanuts.
Make another layer on top, but this time top with a little more cool whip (It takes a large container of cool whip and one jar of ice cream).

Raw Veggie Salad

Jody Coffin
First Assembly of God Church, Rantoul IL

1-cup Splenda
1-Tablespoon vegetable oil
1/4 cup white vinegar
1/4 cup red vinegar

1-cup Green Giant white "shoe-peg" corn (11 ounces)
1-cup sliced carrots
1-cup broccoli
1-cup green pepper
1-cup cauliflower
1-cup celery

Chop vegetables, mix all and marinate 2 hours. This will keep up to 2 weeks in your refrigerator. You can use any veggies you want. I also added a red, a yellow and an orange bell pepper at 1-cup each with extra virgin olive oil and red and white wine vinegars.

Sausage Casserole

Janice Kizer
First Assembly of God Church, Rantoul IL

1-½ pound sausage
12-eggs
3 slices bread torn in small pieces
1 (8 ounce) package cheddar cheese, shredded
1-½ cup milk
Salt and pepper

Brown sausage and drain. Grease a 9x13 inch baking dish. Mix sausage, bread & cheese. Cover bottom of dish with meat mixture. Beat eggs and milk; add salt and pepper. Pour eggs over sausage. Cover with foil and refrigerate until ready to bake.

Bake 45-60 minutes at 350 degrees.

Smothered Pork Chops

Elaine Cler
First Assembly of God Church, Rantoul IL

8-medium size pork chops
2 cans cream of mushroom soup
2 cans milk

Dip chops in flour and fry until golden brown. Place pork chops in 9x13-cake pan. Mix mushroom soup and milk together in a bowl; pour over chops. Cover will foil. Place pan on a sheet pan so it will not boil over into your oven. Bake at 300 degrees for 2-½ hours.

Sweet Potato Casserole (Using canned potatoes)

Sue Ludwig
First Assembly of God Church, Rantoul IL

1-large can sweet potatoes drained and mashed
3 eggs
1-cup evaporated milk
½ cup sugar
1-teaspoon vanilla
½ teaspoon cinnamon

Topping:
½ cup flour
1-cup brown sugar
3/4 stick of soft butter
1-cup crushed corn flakes
Chopped pecans to taste

Cream together potatoes, eggs, milk, sugar, vanilla & cinnamon and pour into greased baking dish. Mix topping ingredients and sprinkle over potato mixture.

Bake at 350 degrees for 45 minutes.

Easy Beef Stroganoff

Carolyn Bramblett
Baptist Church, Calhoun, GA

1-can mushroom soup
½ cup sliced onion
1/3 cup water
2 Tablespoons butter
½ cup sour cream
1-pound round steak cut into strips

In skillet, brown meat. Add remaining ingredients. Cover and simmer for 45 minutes or until meat is tender. Stir now and then. Serve over hot cooked noodles. Serves 4 but recipe can easily be doubled.

Marshmallow Dip

Donna Domanovics
St. Gabriel Church, Ohio

2-7 ounce jars marshmallow cream
1-8 ounce package Philadelphia cream cheese
1-teaspoon almond extract

Cream together. Cover and chill. Serve with a variety of fruits.

Fruit Bars

Joan Krajnak
Cleveland, Ohio

3/4-cup sifted flour
½ teaspoon baking powder
½ teaspoon salt
1-cup firmly packed brown sugar
1/4-cup melted shortening
2-eggs well beaten
1-cup chopped pecans
1-cup chopped dates

Sift together flour, baking powder, salt. Add sugar to dry ingredients and mix well. Combine shortening and eggs. Stir into dry ingredients—blend well. Add nuts and dates. Bake in greased 9-inch square pan until golden brown. Cut into squares while hot. Bake at 350 degrees for 30 minutes.

Rhubarb Preserves

Mary Kruger
Rantoul Christian Church

5 cups fresh rhubarb, diced fine
3-cups sugar
1-(3 ounce) package strawberry Jell-O gelatin

Combine rhubarb and sugar; let stand overnight in refrigerator. The next day bring rhubarb mix to a boil—and let boil for 12 minutes. Remove from heat, add jell-o, stir until dissolved. Pour into clean hot jelly or canning jars and top with wax, canning seals, or just store in refrigerator.

Over-night Salad

Pauline Flick
Rantoul Christian Church

Layer in the following order in a large bowl:
1-head of chopped lettuce
1-head of cauliflower (tips only)
2 cups mayonnaise or miracle whip
1-medium onion chopped
1-pound bacon fried crisp and crumbled
1/3 cup grated parmesan cheese
½ cup sugar

Cover tightly and refrigerate over night. Stir when read to serve.

Round Steak and Gravy

Frank Rose
Anderson California

1-round steak about ½ inch thick
1-can cream of mushroom or celery soup
1-can of water

Cut steak into two—2-½ inch cubes, flour and brown in skillet. Mix 1-can soup and water together. Place browned steak in a casserole dish then add soup and water. Pour over steak, cover with foil. Bake at 350 degrees for about 1 and ½ hours. Check and add more water if needed. When done use the gravy for mashed potatoes, rice or noodles.

Sauerkraut Balls (Appetizers)

Slyvia Ruzek
St. Frances Cabrini, Ohio

2-pounds ground sausage or Italian sweet sausage
½ cup chopped onion
1-large can sauerkraut drained (Do not rinse)
4-Tablespoons bread crumbs (Italian)
1-8 ounce cream cheese
½ teaspoon garlic powder
½ teaspoon pepper

Brown sausage and onion in skillet then drain off the grease. Put cream cheese in sausage and onion mixture until melted. Then add all the ingredients and mix by hand. Break up meat. Refrigerate over night. Take out mixture next day. Make balls in one heaping Tablespoon size. Place on cookie sheet. Heat grease in fryer to 350 degrees. Roll balls into the breading of 4-eggs (beaten) and 12-Tablespoons mil and flour. Drop breaded balls into grease until golden brown. Lay on paper towels.

Low Country Boil

Pat Adamet
St. Malachy Church

8-quarts of water
1/3 cup Crab boil
12-small red new potatoes
1-pound smoked sausage, cut into 4-inch pieces
6 ears fresh corn—broke in half
3 pounds large shrimp (shells on)

In a large Dutch oven, bring water and crab boil to a boil. Add potatoes and sausage; cook for 20 minutes. Add corn; cook for 10 minutes. Stir in shrimp and cook for 3 minutes. Remove from heat and drain well.

Zucchini-Pineapple Bread

Shirley Steffl
St. Casimir, Ohio

3-eggs
1-cup vegetable oil
2-cups sugar
2-cups shredded unpeeled zucchini
1-8 ounce can crushed pineapple with juice
3-cups flour
2-teaspoon cinnamon
1-teaspoon nutmeg
1-½-teaspoon baking soda
½ teaspoon baking powder
1-teaspoon salt
1-cup chopped nuts

In large mixing bowl beat eggs for 30 seconds on low speed. In this order, add oil, sugar, zucchini and pineapple with juice mixing with each addition. Sift dry ingredients together and add to mixture in bowl. Mix on low speed until well blended. Stir in nuts. Pour batter into two greased and floured loaf pans.

Bake at 350 degrees for 50-60 minutes. Cool 10-minutes in pans then turn out on a rack to finish cooling. Makes two large loaves

Mint Melt-a-Way Cake

Pat Adametz
St. Malachy Church, Rantoul

Cake:
1-cup sugar
½ cup margarine
4 eggs
1-teaspoon vanilla
1-can (16 ounces) chocolate syrup
1-cup plus 1-Tablespoon flour

Cream the cake ingredients and bake at 350 degrees for 30 minutes in a 9x13 inch un-greased cake pan.

Icing:

2 drops green food coloring
½ cup margarine
2 cups powdered sugar
2-Tablespoon milk
½ teaspoon peppermint extract
Mix together and spread on cake.

Topping:

6 Tablespoons margarine
1-cup semisweet chocolate chips
Melt slowly on stove or in microwave.
Pour over icing and spread evenly.
Refrigerate.

Pesto Turkey Burgers

Pat Adametz
St. Malachy Church, Rantoul

1-1/4 pounds of ground turkey
1/4 cup pesto (can be found by Spaghetti sauce)
½ cup freshly grated Parmesan
1/3 cup plain bread crumbs
½ teaspoon black pepper

Mix together and form into four burgers. Pan fry or grill until done.

Topping: ½ cup mayonnaise mixed with 1/3 cup diced roasted red peppers

Add red onion slice and greens to burgers.

Rhubarb Dream Bars

Pat Adametz
St. Malachy Church, Rantoul

Crust:
2 cups flour
3/4 cup confectioner (powdered) sugar
1-cup butter or margarine

Filling:
4 eggs
2 cups sugar
½ cup flour
½ teaspoon salt
4 cups thinly sliced fresh rhubarb

Mix crust ingredients together and press into 15x10 inch pan. Bake at 350 degrees for 15 minutes. Combine eggs, sugar, flour and salt; beat together and fold in rhubarb. Spread filling mixture on hot crust. Return to oven to bake 40-45 minutes longer. Cool and cut into bars.

Broccoli Cheese Soup

Connie Frederick
Family of Esther Ross

2 cups chicken broth or bouillon
1-package frozen chopped broccoli
1-cup Velveeta Cheese—1 inch cubes
2 cups milk
Salt & pepper to taste

Cook broccoli in broth, add remaining ingredients and cook until cheese is melted. Serve.

Broccoli Cheese Soup with Onion

Esther Ross
Rantoul Christian Church

2 cans Swanson clear chicken broth (3 of the 1-½ ounce cans)
½ gallon milk
1-stick of butter
1-small onion
½ loaf Velveeta cheese cubed
1-large bunch of broccoli
½ cup cornstarch

Mix broth with finely chopped onion and bite size pieces of broccoli. Cook until broccoli is tender. Add butter and all but 1-½ cups milk. Mix the 1-½ cups of milk with cornstarch and add to broth mixture. Turn burner down and add cubed cheese. Do not boil.

Sex in a Bowl

Pat Adametz
St. Malachy Church, Rantoul

1-(18.25 ounce) light devils food cake mix
2-large egg whites plus 1-large egg
1-1/3 cup water
1/4 cup Kahula or strong brewed coffee

1 (3.9 ounce) chocolate instant pudding
3-cup cold skim milk
½ cup chopped reduced fat chocolate toffee bars (Health bars)
1-8 ounce light cool whip, thawed

Preheat oven to 350 degrees. Combine first four ingredients in a large bowl. Beat at medium speed until well blended. Spoon batter into a 9x13 inch pan coated with cooking spray. Bake for 25 minutes or until toothpick comes out clean. Cool in pan for 10 minutes on a wire rack. Remove from pan. Cool completely on rack. Break into a little larger than bite size pieces.

Combine milk and pudding in a medium bowl. Prepare according to package.
In a large bowl start layers as follows: 1) Put ½ of cake pieces in bowl; 2) Pour half of Kahula over cake pieces; 3) ½ of pudding; 4) ½ of whipped topping and candy pieces. *Repeat layers.* Cover and chill at least 4 hours. Yields 16 servings.

Mandarin Orange Pie

Esther Ross

1-graham cracker crust
1-can mandarin oranges
1-6 ounce can frozen pineapple/orange juice (thaw a little)
9-ounce cool whip

Mix everything together then pour over crust. Cool in refrigerator

Dumplings

Floyd Adophus Studer
Family of Esther Ross

2 cups sifted flour
½ teaspoon salt
1-Tablespoon baking powder
1/8 teaspoon baking soda
½ cup milk

Sift all the dry ingredients together, add milk and stir gently—do not over stir. If mixture is too thick, add a little more milk. Drop by Tablespoons on to simmering liquid. Cook uncovered 10 minutes, cover pot and continue to cook for an additional 15 or 20 minutes. This dumpling recipe is good with stew, soup, or any sweet mixture such as blueberries.

Apple Snicker Salad

Ellen Saveley
Rantoul Christian Church

4-6 red or green delicious apples
1-small instant vanilla pudding
4-Snicker candy bars (or 1-bag miniatures) cut up
1-cup milk
1-8 ounce tub cool whip
Red seedless grapes cut in half

Blend pudding, milk and cool whip together. Dice unpeeled, washed, apples and add to vanilla pudding mixture. Stir in cut up snickers. Refrigerate until ready to serve. Sprinkle some apple pieces, grape halves and snicker chunks on the top of the mixture, and serve.

Barbecue Sauce for Chicken Wings **(Sweet & Sour)**

Esther Ross
Rantoul Christian Church

1-14 ounce bottle catsup
1-8 ounce can tomato sauce
1-cup vinegar
1-teaspoon dry mustard
1-teaspoon ginger
1-cup brown sugar
1-cup white sugar
Dash of Worcester sauce

Cut off tips of chicken wings then cut at joints. Put into one layer in baking dish.

Bake at 350 degrees for 2 hours. Makes enough sauce for 40 wings

Butter Cake

Esther Ross—Rantoul Christian Church

1-cake mix
1-egg
1-stick of butter

1-8 ounce package cream cheese
1-Box powdered sugar
1-teaspoon vanilla
3 eggs
1-can pumpkin
1-stick butter

Mix cake mix, one egg, and the soft stick of butter to form a crust in a 9x13 inch cake pan. Then mix the cream cheese, powdered sugar, vanilla, remaining three eggs, can of pumpkin and stick of soft butter together and pour over crust.

Bake at 350 degrees for 40 minutes.

French Salad Dressing

Cliff Frederick—Family of Esther Ross

1-cup sugar
1-teaspoon salt
1-teaspoon pepper
1-teaspoon dry mustard
1-teaspoon paprika
1-cup salad oil
1-Tablespoon onion salt
1-Tablespoon Worcestershire sauce
½ cup vinegar
1-can tomato soup

Combine all ingredients and blend well. Makes about 1-quart. Keep refrigerated.

Peach Cake

Esther Ross—Rantoul Christian Church

1-can sliced peaches (20 ounces) with juice
1-package cake mix
1-cup nuts (optional)
1-stick margarine melted

Put peaches and juice into 9-13 inch pan. Sprinkle cake mix over peaches. Add nuts on top. Melt margarine and dribble over top. Bake at 350 degrees for 45 minutes. Serve with cool whip. Cherries, pears or any canned berries also work great with this recipe.

Frosting like Whipped Cream

Iva Studer
Family of Esther Ross

5 Tablespoons flour
1-cup milk

Place above ingredients in small pan and cook until smooth paste, let cool. Then beat together:

1-cup butter (certain margarines will cause frosting to not whip)
1-cup sugar
1-teaspoon vanilla

Add cold flour mixture to above mixture and beat until the consistency of whipped cream. Frost cooled cake.

Hot Taco Salad

Esther Ross
Rantoul Christian Church

1-½ pound ground beef
1-cup green peppers (optional)
1-large onion chopped
1-Tablespoon chili powder
6-8 dashes cumin powder
1-package taco seasoning
1-pound Velveeta cheese
1-can hot chili beans or pork & beans
1-can Enchilada mild sauce
1-can Italian tomatoes
Garlic, salt & pepper to taste

Put this in a crock-pot to heat. In another bowl tear apart a head of lettuce, add chopped tomatoes and a 6 ounce can (or bag) of chips. When ready to eat pour hot mixture over lettuce and serve.

Rice Casserole

Kyle Saveley
Rantoul Christian Church

1-stick margarine cut up
2 cups minute rice
1-can onion soup
1-can consommé soup
Salt and pepper
Optional: mushrooms, celery and/or green peppers

Mix all the above in a baking dish. Bake at 350 degrees for 60 minutes. Yields 8 servings

Meal in a Bowl Chicken Soup

Cheryl Scheffer—Family of Esther Ross

6 cups chicken broth
1-cup sliced carrots
1-cup sliced celery
1-cup sliced onion
1-cup frozen peas & corn
2 cups shredded cooked chicken
1-cup cooked macaroni twists, shells or pasta
2 Tablespoons parsley
Salt & pepper to taste

Bring broth to a boil in a 4-quart saucepan. Add carrots, celery, and onion. Simmer 8 minutes or until crisp tender. Add peas, corn, and chicken. Cover and simmer 4 minutes or until done. Add rest of ingredients, heat and serve.

Mini Chicken Pot Pies

Ginny Ratts
Rantoul Christian Church, Rantoul IL

1-½ cups frozen peas and carrots
1-cup cubed (½ inch pieces) cooked chicken
1-cup refrigerated diced cooked potatoes with onions (from 20 ounce bag)
1/4 cup milk
½ teaspoon dried thyme leaves
1-can (10-3/4 ounce) condensed cream of chicken soup
1-can (4 ounce) Pillsbury refrigerated crescent rolls
1-egg
1-Tablespoon water
1/8 teaspoon dried thyme leaves

Pre-heat oven to 400 degrees. In a 2-quart sauce pan—mix peas & carrots, chicken, potatoes, milk, ½ teaspoon thyme and soup; Heat to boiling over medium heat, stirring occasionally. Divide mixture evenly among four ungreased 10-ounce custard cups. Unroll crescent dough. Place crescent over each custard cup. In a small bowl mix egg and water; brush mixture over crescent dough. Sprinkle 1/4 teaspoon thyme over dough.

Bake 11-13 minutes or until crusts are golden brown.

*   *   *

*"What we are is God's gift to us.
What we become is our gift to God."
~ Eleanor Powell*

Licketty—Split Lasagna

Ginny Ratts
Rantoul Christian Church, Rantoul IL

3/4 pound ground beef
2-½ cup spaghetti sauce
6 dried lasagna noodles (uncooked)
1-½ cup cream-style cottage cheese
1-½ cup shredded mozzarella cheese (6 ounce)
2-Tablespoons grated Parmesan cheese (optional)

In large skillet cook ground beef over med heat until brown. Drain fat. Spoon 1-cup spaghetti sauce into bottom of 2-quart rectangular baking dish. Stir remaining sauce into meat in skillet. Cook over med heat until heated through out, stirring occasionally. Place 2-uncooked noodles in the sauce in dish. Spread 1/3 meat mixture on top of noodles then spread ½ of cottage cheese over meat. Sprinkle ½ cup mozzarella cheese over cottage cheese. Add another layer of noodles, 1/3 meat mixture, remaining cottage cheese and ½ cup mozzarella cheese. Layer remaining noodles, meat mixture and mozzarella. If desired sprinkle with parmesan cheese. Cover dish with foil. Bake at 350 degrees for 1-hour. Place covered dish on wire rack. Let stand 15 minutes before serving. (Makes 6 servings)

Oat Meal Patties

Esther Ross
Rantoul Christian Church

2 cups oatmeal
1-cup corn flakes
2 eggs
1-Tablespoon sage
1-cup chopped onions
½ Tablespoon flour
2 Tablespoons oil
½ cup milk

2 cups water
3 Tablespoons Soya sauce

Mix all but water and Soya sauce together. Make into patties. Fry on both sides until brown. Mix 2 cups water and 3 Tablespoons Soya sauce and pour over patties. Cook slowly until liquid is gone.

*   *   *

"In the childhood memories of every good cook, there's a large kitchen, a warm stove, a simmering pot and a mom."
~ Barbara Costikyan

Pineapple Angel Food Pie

Pauline Flick
Rantoul Christian Church

1-can crushed pineapple with juice
3/4 cup sugar
1/4 teaspoon salt
½ cup water

Bring all this to a boil. Mix 3 Tablespoons cornstarch in ½ cup water and thicken the above ingredients with mixture. Cool.

3 egg whites
Pinch of salt
1/4 cup sugar
1-teaspoon vanilla

Beat in metal or glass bowl until stiff. Then fold into the above mixture. Pour into a baked pie shell. Refrigerate and top with whipped cream when ready to serve.

Pineapple Sponge Salad

Pauline Flick
Rantoul Christian Church

4 packages Knox plain gelatin
1-large can crushed pineapple
2-½ cup sugar
1-pint whipping cream
½ pint cold water
1-½ pint boiling water
1-½ teaspoon lemon juice
Red Maraschino Cherries
3-4 Tablespoons cherry juice

Dissolve gelatin in cold water in large bowl. Add pineapple and juice. Add boiling water and sugar to mixture. Stir until sugar dissolves. Let stand in refrigerator until set like jell-o. Take out and stir up. Beat whipping cream until stiff and add to jell-o mixture. Cut up cherries and add with juice to mixture. Use as many cherries as you like. The cherry juice makes it light pink. Refrigerate until ready to serve.

*   *   *

The life I touch for good or ill will touch another
life, and that in turn another, until who knows
where the trembling stops or in what far place my
touch will be felt. ~ Frederick Buechner

Poor Mans Homemade Soup

Connie Frederick—Family of Esther Ross

3 cups water
1 or 2 onions—chopped
1-pound hamburger
2 cans diced tomatoes
Whole kernel corn, carrots, celery
Macaroni

Cook hamburger in water. Add onions, potatoes, whole kernel corn, macaroni, carrots and celery. Cook until vegetables are tender. Season with salt and pepper; or any of your favorite seasonings.

Seafood Salad

Esther Ross—Rantoul Christian Church

1-box of macaroni
2 pounds artificial flaked crabmeat
2 cups diced celery
2 cups mayonnaise (not salad dressing)
½ teaspoon white pepper
½ teaspoon dill-weed
6 hard boiled eggs—chopped
1-diced red or green pepper

This recipe makes a lot of salad so Esther likes to cut it in half and share it with her sister and family.

Spaghetti Sauce for large crowd or for canning

Eunice Nichols—Family of Esther Ross

½-bushel of peeled tomatoes
1-clump garlic
3-green peppers
1-cup onion—diced
1-cup celery—diced
2-Tablespoons salt
4-cups sugar
1-cup vegetable oil
3-cans tomato paste
1-½ cups parmesan cheese
1-Tablespoon cayenne pepper
1-Tablespoon parsley flakes
4-Tablespoons *each*—thyme, basil, oregano
½ Tablespoon mono sodium glutamate
1-Tablespoon *each*—paprika, garlic powder, onion powder, crushed red pepper

Put all the vegetables, including the peeled tomatoes, through a blender. Add all other ingredients and simmer until desired thickness. Fill canning jars and process jars with seals in a water bath for at least 30 minutes. This recipe makes between 15 to 20 quarts.

Sticky Buns

Esther Ross—Rantoul Christian Church
Studer Family Recipe

2 loaves of frozen bread
2 boxes vanilla pudding (not instant)
1-stick margarine
1-cup brown sugar
½ teaspoon cinnamon
2-Tablespoons milk

Use 9x13 inch glass cake pan. Take first loaf of bread and tear into little balls, covering the bottom of the pan. Mix all remaining ingredients together and pour over the first loaf of bread. Tear the second loaf of bread into little balls and place between the other balls in the pan. Bake for 20 minutes at 350 degrees.

Texas Hot Sauce

Bethany Peet—Family of Esther Ross

½ pound of ground meat—cooked and drained
Add:
1-cup tomato soup
1 scant cup water
½ teaspoon paprika
½ teaspoon dry mustard
1-Tablespoon Worcestershire sauce
1 minced onion
½ teaspoon sugar
2 bay leaves
1-Tablespoon chili powder

Season to taste with salt, black pepper, red pepper & ground cloves. Slow cook until thick; remove the bay leaves & serve on hot dogs.

Turkey Burgers

Bethany Peet
Family of Esther Ross

1 small can chick peas—drained & mashed
1-beaten egg
2 Tablespoons bread crumbs
1-½ teaspoons Cajun seasoning
1-pound ground turkey or chicken

Mix all ingredients together, shape into patties and broil 3 to 4 inches from broiler for 6 minutes. Turn, broil 6 to 8 minutes other side. Butter & toast rolls under broiler, add lettuce, tomato & mayonnaise if desired.

Texas Style Deep Dish Chili Pie

Ginny Ratts—Rantoul Christian Church

1-pound hamburger or stew meat cut up small
2-cans (14-½ ounce each) stewed tomatoes un-drained (Mexican for hotter sauce)
1-medium green bell pepper diced
1-package (1.25 ounce) Lawry's Taco Seasoning
1-Tablespoon yellow cornmeal
1-can (15-1/4 ounce) kidney beans, drained
1-package (15 ounce) flat refrigerated pie crusts
½-cup shredded cheddar cheese divided

In Dutch oven brown beef and drain fat. Add stewed tomatoes, bell pepper, taco seasonings and cornmeal. Bring to boil, reduce heat and simmer uncovered 20-minutes. Add kidney beans. In 10-inch pie plate un-fold 1-crust; fill with chili mixture and 1/4 cup cheese. Top with remaining crust—fluting edges. Bake uncovered in 350 degree oven for 30-minutes. Sprinkle remaining cheese over crust and return to oven and bake 10-minutes longer. (Serves 6)

Three Bean Baked Beans

Esther Ross—Rantoul Christian Church

1-can butter beans
1-can baked beans
1-can kidney beans
½ pound bacon fried & drained
1-pound hamburger fried with large onion
1-cup brown sugar
1-cup catsup
1-Tablespoon molasses
1-Tablespoon vinegar

Bake 1-hour at 350 degrees.

Up-side-down Meat Loaf

Esther Ross—Rantoul Christian Church

½ cup brown sugar
1-½ pound hamburger
2 eggs
1-onion (chopped)
3/4 cup bread crumbs
½ cup catsup
3/4 cup milk
1-teaspoon salt
1/4 teaspoon pepper
1/4 teaspoon ginger

Mix all ingredients together. Put into buttered baking dish and bake at 350 degrees for 1-hour and 30 minutes.

Turkey Chili—No Fat

Esther Ross—Rantoul, IL

1 package of ground white turkey breast or 1-1/4 pound—no fat
1-16 ounce can kidney or pinto beans—undrained
1-16 ounce can stewed tomatoes
1-6 ounce can tomato paste
1-can tomato soup
2 Tablespoons chili powder
2 Tablespoons dried onion
½ teaspoon garlic powder
½ teaspoon oregano
½ teaspoon cumin
½ teaspoon paprika
½ teaspoon black pepper
½ teaspoon salt

Cook turkey in just enough water to keep meat from sticking to pan. Add rest of ingredients plus 1-½ to 2 cups of water. Stir thoroughly. Cook over medium heat 15 to 30 minutes. It is real good over spaghetti. Only don't put that much water in sauce for spaghetti. Make it thicker.

Spaghetti Pie

Barb Lankford—Rantoul, IL

6-ounces spaghetti noodles
2 teaspoons butter
1/3 cup grated parmesan cheese
2 beaten eggs
1-cup cottage cheese
1-pound ground beef
½ cup chopped onion
1-(6 ounce) can tomato paste
1-(8 ounce) can tomatoes
1-teaspoon sugar
1-teaspoon dried oregano
½ teaspoon garlic salt
½ cup shredded mozzarella
1/4 cup chopped green peppers

Cook spaghetti, drain, stir in butter, parmesan cheese and eggs. Form spaghetti mixture into a crust in buttered pie plate. Spread cottage cheese over bottom of crust. Brown the beef and add onions and green peppers until tender. Drain. Stir in un-drained tomatoes, tomato paste, sugar, oregano and garlic salt. Heat through. Pour meat mixture into the crust. Bake uncovered at 350 degrees for 20 minutes. Sprinkle mozzarella cheese on top. Bake 5 minutes longer or until cheese melts. Makes 6 servings (Barb notes: When in a hurry use your favorite prepared spaghetti sauce with the meat.)

Kids Can Cook Too

Rhiannon Hogard's Pumpkin Bars

Bright and bubbly 10 years old Rhiannon Hogard, of Rantoul, Illinois, shines of her Sicilian heritage. Rhiannon loves to be in the kitchen and dreams of becoming a pastry chef.

Tari Kinsel says her daughter has had a love for cooking since she was just two years old. "She loved to watch Emeril Lagasse on the Food Network channel." It was from there that show she picked up a "Bam (!)" of excitement for baking. (For those of you that don't know—that is how Emeril opens his show—"Bam (!)"

Some of Rhiannon's earliest and most cherished memories are those spent helping her grandma Linda Zarnsy bake cookies. "I loved licking the spoon," Rhiannon said.

Rhiannon's bright eyes and dazzling smile light up an entire room and draw you in. Her enthusiasm for life is priceless.

Rhiannon proudly admits that she has always done very well in school. "My favorite classes are Math and Reading," Rhiannon says. "I like Science too," explaining that there is a lot of science in cooking.

Rhiannon was in the 4th grade at Broadmeadow in Rantoul when I wrote this story about her as a column for the Rantoul Press in September 2007, but she continues working diligently to get as many A's as she possible can.

Although Rhiannon is a typical child that loves to play with her friends and kick a soccer ball around, she is quite exceptional in her mother's eyes. Rhiannon helps her mom a lot by cooking meals for her younger siblings—Morgan and Jackson. She especially enjoys cooking up pancakes, eggs and bacon for them.

Although she likes cooking up breakfast for her siblings, she is actually quite famous for her Pumpkin Bars.

In June of 2006, Rhiannon's grandma Linda Zarnsy became quite ill. Due to a rare blood condition, her grandma Linda needed a new liver and had to under go surgery. Rhiannon wanted to help the family in caring for Grandma asking if she could bake something for her.

Tari explained that her mom (Linda Zarnsy) had received some food assistance through the Community Service Center, "So I gave Rhiannon a can of pumpkin that was with the food commodities and turned her lose in the kitchen."

Rhiannon was just 8 years old at the time. Now when she bakes her infamous Pumpkin Bars everybody wants them. They are unbelievably moist and delicious! Bless her little heart for sharing her recipe us.

Pumpkin Bars

4-eggs 2-teaspoons baking powder
1-2/3 cup of sugar 2-teaspoons cinnamon
1-cup oil 1-teaspoon baking soda
1-15 ounce can pumpkin (NOT pie mix) Pinch of salt
2-cups all purpose flour

Preheat your oven to 350 degrees. Cream the eggs and sugar together, then add the oil and pumpkin. Mix well. Sift all the dry ingredients together and then mix in with the pumpkin batter. Spread your mixture into a well-greased 13x9 inch baking dish and back for 30 minutes. Cool completely and ice.

Icing: 8-ounces cream cheese, ½ cup butter, 2-cups powdered sugar, 1-teaspoon vanilla extract

When the cream cheese and butter come to room temperature and are soft—mix with sugar and vanilla and spread on cooled Pumpkin Bars.—Did you know that the pinch of salt you add to deserts, especially chocolates, enhances the flavor? I did not know that. I add salt because the recipe says to do so. Thanks to Rhiannon I am a bit wiser.

Fudge Cycles

First Assembly of God Church, Rantoul IL

1 Box Chocolate Instant Pudding
1/4 cup sugar
1/4 cup cream
Add milk as box calls for then pour into molds and freeze.

Pop Cycles—No drip

First Assembly of God Church, Rantoul IL

1-package Jell-O any flavor
1-package Kool-aid
1-cup sugar
2-cups hot water
Mix together—then add 2 cups cold water. Makes 20 no drip cycles.

Fruit Drink Pops

First Assembly of God Church, Rantoul IL

6 Tablespoons fruit flavored drink mix
2-Tablespoons sugar
1-1/4 cups water
Dissolve drink mix and sugar in water. Pour into molds, seal and freeze.

Banana Yogurt Pops

First Assembly of God Church, Rantoul IL

2 bananas
2 ounces plain yogurt
1/4 cup milk
1-Tablespoon sugar if desired
Break bananas into chunks & place in a small bowl. Mash thoroughly with a fork then add the yogurt. Blend in the milk & sugar. Pour into molds, seal and freeze.

Fruit Juice Pops

First Assembly of God Church, Rantoul IL

1-6 ounce frozen concentrate fruit juice—any flavor
1-6 ounce can of water
Mix together and pour into molds, seal and freeze.

Good Pop

First Assembly of God Church, Rantoul IL

2 envelopes instant breakfast drink mix, any flavor
1-1/3 cups milk
In small bowl stir milk into powdered mix, blend well. Pour into molds, seal
& freeze.

Play Dough

Harriet Cotter—Rantoul, IL

2-cups flour
1-cup salt
1/4 cup vegetable oil
1-cup warm water
4-Tablespoon cream of tartar

Mix well; add food coloring of your choice. Keep stored in an air tight container.

Play Dough

Mary's Step-daughter Lorna Kruger—Rossville, IL

2-cup flour
½ cup salt
2 teaspoons cream of tarter
1-cup water
1-Tablespoon vegetable oil and Food Color of choice

Cook together over medium heat till well mixed; let cool a bit before using. Keep stored in an air tight container.

Snicker Doodles

Mary's Step daughter—Kelly Kruger—Rantoul, IL

1-cup soft shortening—part butter
1-½ cup sugar
2-eggs
2-3/4 cup flour
2-teaspoon cream of tartar
1-teaspoon baking soda
1/4 teaspoon salt

Preheat oven to 400 degrees. Mix shortening, sugar, and eggs thoroughly. Blend all dry ingredients. Roll into balls the size of small walnuts. Roll in mixture of 2-teaspoons sugar and 2-teaspoons cinnamon. Bake for 8-10 minutes on un-greased cookies sheet placing cookies 2 inches a part. Makes 5 dozen

Movie Star Muffins

Mary's Step daughter—Kaylynn Kruger
Rantoul, IL

4-Tablespoons melted butter
½ teaspoon salt
1/3 cup sugar
½ cup milk
1-egg (well beaten)
3/4 cup chopped sour cherries (drain if necessary)
1-½ cups sifted flour
2-½ teaspoons baking powder

Preheat oven to 400 degrees. Cream butter and sugar; add sifted dry ingredients and add—alternating with the milk. Add cherries. Mix well and spoon into greased muffin tins. Bake for 20-24 minutes. [Note from Kaylynn—HIDE the cherries so your little sister doesn't eat them first!]

My step-daughter Layne Kruger was just eight years old when she began chemotherapy treatment for her ITP (Idiopathic Thrombocytopenic Purpura). ITP is an immune disorder in which the body attacks the cells responsible for blood clotting (platelets). The cause of ITP is not known. But people with this disorder may have bruises or black-and-blue marks on the skin. Some cases of ITP may go away on their own and do not require treatment, but in Layne's case—she needed treatment to control the bleeding. The Chemo treatments Layne received made her very nauseous and sick. One of the nurses at Carle said she had heard that homemade vanilla pudding helps to settle the stomach and gave us this recipe to try. It was amazing. For each treatment there after I prepared Layne this pudding—which she thoroughly enjoyed—and it stopped her vomiting. This recipe—this experience—inspired the title for this book "The Proof is in the Pudding".

Vanilla Cornstarch Pudding

From Nurse Sarah for Layne Kruger
Carle Clinic Cancer Treatment Center, Champaign IL

4 cups milk—scalded
2/3 cup sugar
1/3 cup cornstarch
Dash of salt
2 eggs, beaten
1/4 cup milk
1-teaspoon vanilla

Combine the sugar, cornstarch, salt, eggs, and 1/4 cup milk—mixing till smooth. Add mixture to the scaled milk stirring continuously (on medium burner) with a wire wisp until thick. Remove from heat and add vanilla. Stir and serve warm or refrigerate and serve chilled.

Moms and Grandmothers

"Laugh and the world laughs with you; cry and you cry alone . . ." (Ma—Connie Denault)

I'm sure those words belong to someone else, but somehow as a child I was certain my mother owned them.

A beautiful and dedicated woman, so full of life and love, my mom was the Lucile Ball of central Illinois. You just couldn't help but adore her.

Born and raised a city girl, bound for college with her remarkable artistic talents, mom meets farmer and trades in her paint brush and easel for broom sticks, cookbooks and a bakers dozen of children; a tapestry of two entirely different worlds.

Grandma taught my Ma a lot about cooking and sewing, but it was her love for books and reading that gave her the wisdom and knowledge she needed to adapt to farm life. But it wasn't until she read various farm-wife magazines that she would start wearing those colorful aprons with diaper pins dangling from their fancy pockets.

Watching Ma flip fresh homemade noodles over clothes hangers to dry was quite an amazing feat. With pasta dangling from the doors and doorways while she created her strange concoctions would lead one to believe she might have been some kind of scientist in a former life.

She would take stuff like stale soda crackers and peanut butter—along with a few other miscellaneous secret ingredients and turn it into candy. Left over mashed potatoes became delicious bread and doughnuts.

Mom learned early on that a farmer's wife had to have the faith of a nun. There wasn't a day went by she wasn't asking the good Lord to help her weather some kind of incredible storm us kids, or the animals or her farmer husband was getting into. Often times her prayer became a song.

Now keep in mind, my mother is an artist. Not a singer. Not a song writer. So inevitably when she sang the world around her came to a screeching halt. The woman could not carry a tune. But when the kids got out of control, she would sing her heart out. And within seconds, a dozen or so bodies would stop,

169

drop and roll—in laughter. With sides splitting we would totally forget what we had all been arguing about.

I remember some really special chats we all had with Ma in the kitchen while Dad was busy running errands in town. We'd gather around the table sharing jokes or funny stories as we gobbled up Ma's fresh home baked chocolate chip cookies. It was magical how that aroma brought us all together.

And it was mystical how her gentle whisper, "Your Dad's home," could get us back to our stations so quickly. Dad was the lightening. We were the thunder.

Scattering in every direction, the girls would grab a basket of clothes to fold, or a broom, or vacuum or dust rag while the boys would head for the back bedroom. That's right, the room with the window closest to the ground. The one they could make their escape into the great out doors through. It was important they at least looked like they'd been busy with their farm chores while dad was away.

"When you laugh, the world laughs with you . . ." Thanks Ma! Your rug rats are all grown up now—but you are not forgotten. Thanks for keeping my faith alive Momma, and for the many years of love and laughter. You're the best!

Root Beer

Ma—Connie Denault
Bourbonnais, IL

Pour one 3-ounce bottle root beer extract over 4-pounds sugar. Mix well. Add 4-3/4 gallons of lukewarm water and dissolve sugar. Add ½ teaspoon dry yeast to 1-cup luke warm water and add to rest. Mix well and bottle immediately; filling jars or pop bottles to ½ inch of top. Lay bottles on their sides in a warm place away from drafts for 5 days. Cool & drink.

Ma used to use an old cream separator; she says "It's perfect because of the spigot, which fills pop bottles so well. Pop bottles work best but you will need a capper and caps."

Cherry Almond Pie

Ma—Connie Denault

1-can sour red cherries
½ cup water
2 Tablespoons cornstarch
3/4 cup sugar
1-Tablespoon butter
1-teaspoon almond extract
½ teaspoon red food color

Drain juice and bring to boil, add cornstarch dissolved in cold water and sugar. Cook until thick and clear. Add cherries and the rest. Put into baked crust and chill.
Serve with whipped cream or ice cream.

Cowboy Coffee Cake

Ma—Connie Denault

2-½ cups flour
½ teaspoon salt
2-cups brown sugar
2/3 cup shortening
2-teaspoons baking powder
½ teaspoon soda
½ teaspoon cinnamon
½ teaspoon nutmeg
1-cup sour milk
2-well beaten eggs
Chopped nuts

Mix flour, salt, sugar and shortening until crumbly. Save ½ cup for topping. To rest add baking powder, soda, and spices. Mix well. Add milk and eggs. Mix. Pour into a well greased 8-inch pan. Sprinkle with the saved chopped nuts & cinnamon. Bake at 375 degrees for 25-30 minutes.

Kneeblatz ("Knee Patches" taste like Elephant Ears)

Ma—Connie Denault—Bourbonnais, IL

I remember momma making these knee patches every summer as I was growing up. It was a lot of work to make enough to feed the 14 of us kids, but Ma was very dedicated to making enjoyable treats that all of us would enjoy. They were especially great when we got stuck working on the farm and missing out on the carnivals that came to town. At least with the homemade Kneeblatz we felt like we were there.

Kneeblatz
3-eggs
½ teaspoon salt
1-cup cream
Enough flour to make stiff dough.

Mix by rolling and knead on floured board until blisters appear. Roll golf ball size piece of dough out as thin as possible. Gently place into hot deep fat fryer oil. If too big for fryer stick a fork into the middle of dough and twist after placed into the oil. Fry until golden brown. Sprinkle generously with sugar and stack in a large tin or paper grocery sack.

Baker's Meringue

Ma—Connie Denault

Mix about 2 teaspoons water with 1 Tablespoon cornstarch
Add ½ cup boiling water and cook until thick and clear. Cool well.
Beat 3 egg whites until stiff and add a few grains of salt and 6 Tablespoons sugar.
Beat in the cooled cornstarch mix until it stands in pretty peaks. Spread on
pie of choice and bake at 375 degrees or until brown.

This was one of David (Dr.) Kruger's favorite meals as a child. David's
Grandmother Pauline Kruger handed it down to her daughter-in-law
Harriet, (David's mom), back in the early 1950's. And truth be known—he
still enjoys it today.

Homemade Macaroni and Cheese

Harriet Kruger from her Mother-in-law Pauline Kruger

2-cups cooked macaroni noodles
1-cup sharp cheddar cheese—cubed
½ cup milk
1-3/4 cup tomato juice
2-½ Tablespoons sugar
2-Tablespoons butter
Dash of salt

Put cooked/drained macaroni in a baking dish; add cheese, milk, sugar, butter and salt. Stir together. Add tomato juice and stir again. Bake in oven at 400 degrees for about 45 minutes or until top is brown. *Note: If tomato juice causes a curdling affect do not worry. You didn't do anything wrong. It's okay. Just continue to stir and bake.

Frosting

Mother-in-law Harriet Kruger—Muncie, Indiana

2 cups milk
10 Tablespoons flour
2 cups butter or margarine
2 cups powdered sugar sifted
2 teaspoons vanilla

Cook milk and flour until thick. Cool and place in refrigerator until later.

Blend together with mixer the margarine, powdered sugar and vanilla. Add flour-milk mixture a little at a time. Ice cake a layer at a time.

Waldorf-Astoria Red Velvet Cake

Mother-in-law Harriet Kruger—Muncie, Indiana

Although the details are sketchy at best, red velvet cake is not as Southern as many like to think. The story, which began circulating some time in the 1940s, claimed that Manhattan's elegant Waldorf-Astoria granted a diner's request for the recipe, and then a short time later sent her a bill in the amount of $100. The angry woman, apparently with revenge in mind, then began circulating the recipe along with the story. Harriet remembers getting her recipe very discretely from her step-mom Lena Hamilton in the late 1950's.

Waldorf Red Velvet Cake

½ cup Crisco
1-½ cup sugar
2 eggs
1/4 cup red food coloring (or 4 Tablespoons)
2 Tablespoons baking cocoa
1-teaspoon salt
1-teaspoon vanilla
1-cup buttermilk
2-1/4 cup flour (sifted 2 or 3 times)
1-Tablespoon vinegar
1-teaspoon soda

Preheat oven to 350°F. Grease and flour two 9-inch cake pans; cream Crisco and sugar until very fluffy. Add eggs. Beat one minute. Put cocoa and red coloring in a cup to make paste. Add to the Crisco and sugar. Add salt. Put vanilla in buttermilk. Add slowly with flour alternating each. Put vinegar and soda in a cup and mix. Put in with the rest and do not mix—just blend.

Pour equal portions of batter in each cake pan. Bake for 25-30 minutes. Cool on cake rack. Then split layers with a thread to create four layers.

~ In Loving Memory of Norma Gadbois ~
Grandmother of my nine—Stephanie, Joshua, Veronica, Jessica, Jeremiah, Sarah, Theresa, and Joseph

Norma loved to cook for her grandchildren—always remembering their favorite dishes. There are many recipes she will be remembered for but her Turtle Cake was one that will live on in her memory forever. Grandpa Ray will especially remember this one because he always got to un-wrap the whole bag of caramels. And guess what? The cake tasted just fine without those few missing caramels. You know—the ones we all just *know* he ate! ~ We love you grandpa and know you are missing grandma terribly. ~

Turtle Cake

Grandma—Norma Gadbois
Kankakee, IL

1-Betty Crocker German Chocolate Cake Mix
14 ounce package caramels
3/4 cup butter or margarine
½ cup evaporated milk
6 ounce package chocolate chips (or 1-cup)
1-½ cups chopped pecans

Grease and flour a 9x13 inch baking dish. Mix cake mix according to box directions. Pour half the cake batter into baking dish and bake for 15 minutes at 350 degrees. While baking that part of the cake melt (unwrapped) caramels with the butter and milk on a medium burner—stirring often. Pour mixture over warm cake. Sprinkle with chocolate chips and top with pecans. Pour the rest of the batter over that and bake for another 20 minutes at 350 degrees. Top with cool whip or ice cream and serve warm or chilled.

Meat Loaf

Ma—Connie Denault

3/4-pound hamburger
1/4-pound sausage
1-slightly eaten egg
1-small onion grated
Dash pepper
½ teaspoon salt
½ teaspoon sage
2-Tablespoons chopped celery
1/4 teaspoon dry mustard
½ teaspoon Worcestershire sauce

Mix all ingredients together well. Form into a loaf or loaf pan and cover with following sauce: 3-Tablespoons brown sugar, 1-teaspoon mustard, Dash nutmeg, 1/4 cup catsup Bake at 350 degrees for 1 hour.

I love being in my kitchen but I seriously dislike having to plan meals. So when I heard about the SHARE program it was like finding a new best friend. I did not have to plan any more meals. YA-HOO! Each month I get excited to pick up my pre-boxed groceries along with a news-paper filled with awesome recipe ideas. It's good quality—inexpensive food and I don't even have to carry them to the car. When was the last time someone carried your groceries to the car for you? What many do not realize is that it is not just for low income families. It is for everyone. In fact—the more people who utilize the program the more affective it is. So even if you don't do it for your own personal pleasure you can do it to insure it will be available for others—especially seniors and those on a fixed income.

SHARE Foods

"If you eat—you qualify"

Tired of planning your meals? Needing some help with the food budget? Then let S.H.A.R.E. (Self-Help and Resource Exchange) Foods assist you. For just $18 dollars a month and two volunteer hours—which you are probably already doing—you can receive fresh fruits, vegetables, and meats—along with tasty recipes to help you in preparing your meals.

The *Rantoul Loving Action SHARE Food* program would love to share food with your hungry tummy. Everyone is welcomed to join this program.

S.H.A.R.E., is a non-governmental, community development program whose purpose is to enable people, who believe in self-help, to work together to meet their needs of quality, healthy food at an affordable price.

S.H.A.R.E. upholds the self-respect and dignity of people. Everyone is important. There is no one-way transfer of anything. Being a participant in this food program is not charity because each participant gives two hours a month of volunteer service to the community.

It's so simple. Volunteer time is based on an honor system. A person could do such things as pick up trash in their neighborhood or park. They could call on a sick or elderly neighbor or baby-sit for a single mom or family that needs some time out. It could mean spending time with a teen in need of a little attention. The sick and those confined to their homes can pray for a couple hours a month for the hungry of the world.

S.H.A.R.E. is that of community. We are all in it together and the continued success of this program depends upon and demands a sense of shared purpose. Without an active number of participants those needing the program the most will be the ones to suffer.

Many of our elderly and disabled friends and neighbors have come to depend on S.H.A.R.E. Foods. But—it can only continue if the community gets actively involved. This is a program where everyone—whether employed or unemployed—is eligible to participate.

If you haven't tried it—you can sign up at the Community Service Center, 520 E. Wabash Ave, Rantoul IL or call 217-892-4452. If you have tried it in previous years and maybe weren't satisfied for some reason or another—try it again. They have vastly improved the program.

What I love about this program is the neat tips and recipes that come with the food. The University of Illinois Extension in co-operation with SHARE Food sends out recipes as well as tips to go along with the food that is being distributed for that month. You can't go wrong! There is even free delivery to the home bound and seniors.

In one News Bulletin some of the items receive for the month were listed as: pre-cooked meat entrée, fully cooked chicken tacos, "Tilapia" Fish Fillets, ham steak, fresh red potatoes, onions, baby carrots, lettuce, broccoli/slaw mix, radishes, apples, bananas, and pears. And it's different each month.

Some of the recipes included that month were Tilapia & sweet corn baked in foil, pan fried Tilapia, ham and hash brown casserole, ham and rice bake, cheesy ham casserole, grilled potato salad, onion-roasted potatoes, broccoli slaw, Uncle Bill's Microwave Potato Chips, Orange-Glazed Carrots & sugar snap peas, Hawaiian Salad, Pear Waldorf Salad, and Apple Cinnamon Coffee Cake.

It's healthy! It's nourishing! It's an opportunity to put the family back into the kitchen again! Imagine that!

If meat is not your thing then sign up for the fresh produce for $9.00. It's a win-win situation! You get great meal ideas and more time for the family while helping others to help themselves.

If you eat—you qualify! Please help keep the S.H.A.R.E. Food program alive in this community! If you have any questions or problems please feel free to call 217-892-4452.

*   *   *

There was a time in my life when I was the one needing the help. When I humbly waited in line to receive a food basket or voucher help to pay a heating bill. I experienced first hand just how valuable each can of soup collected for food distribution really is. Amazingly enough—the following recipe is one of my children's favorite meals and it was created out of necessity. From the bags of donated food came boxes of saltine crackers and numerous cans of tuna. The SHARE (Self Help and Resource Exchange) program which I was involved in offered fresh vegetables especially fresh onions. So together with those foods and an old Salmon Patty recipe of my mothers and substituting tuna for salmon I created a very delicious and nutritious tuna patty recipe. It was a wonderful way of not only stretching a can of tuna but glorifying it.

Mary's Tuna Patties

Mary Kruger

1-can of tuna (in oil works best) drained
1-egg
1-small diced onion
10-12 saltine crackers (hand crushed)
Salt & Pepper to season

I would take 6-8 cans of drained tuna—and remember, I was preparing a meal for nine children back then. For every can of tuna add 1-egg, 1-small onion diced, and 10-12 crushed saltines.

The trick is to mix the tuna, egg and onions together while waiting on your grill or electric skillet to heat up. Once the grill & oil is hot you'll mix your crumbled crackers into the tuna mix. Mixing them too early and letting them sit will cause them to get soggy and not taste as crisp.

Using an ice cream scoop (or form into patties) gently drop onto the hot oil covered grill one scoop at a time. With the rounded side of the spoon or scoop flatten your patties to about one half inch thickness and let cook until crisp on the bottom side. Season with salt and pepper then carefully turn your patties over; adding a couple more Tablespoons of oil to the grill if needed and cook until opposite side is crisp. Then serve immediately with melted cheese, fresh broccoli or peas, and mashed potatoes or rice. Yield: 2 servings per can of tuna

Cabbage Coleslaw

University of Illinois Extension, Champaign IL
April 2008 (SHARE Food Newsletter Insert)

1-small head of cabbage, shredded
1-small onion, diced
1-cup grated carrot
1-teaspoons celery seed
½ cup sugar
½ cup vinegar
1/3 cup cooking oil
Salt & pepper to taste

In a medium bowl combine cabbage, onion, carrot and celery seed. Sprinkle sugar over cabbage mixtures and mix well. In a small saucepan, combine vinegar and oil. Bring to a boil. Pour hot vinegar and oil over cabbage mixture and mix well; salt & pepper to taste. Serve immediately or chill. Store in refrigerator—Serves 10

[Nutrition facts per serving: calories 130, fat 8 g, calories from fat 70, sodium 35 mg, total carbohydrate 16 g, fiber 2 g]

Ham and Sweet Potato Dinner

University of Illinois Extension, Champaign IL
November 2007 (SHARE Food Newsletter Insert)

1-½ pounds sliced cooked ham
1-cup pineapple juice
½ cup softened raisins
½ cup brown sugar
4-sweet potatoes, partially cooked, peeled & cut in half
8-pineapple slices

To soften raisins place in a small bowl and cover with hot water, let sit 15-20 minutes & drain. To partially cook sweet potatoes—pierce and cook whole in the microwave on high for 5-8 minutes or in the conventional oven at 375 degrees for 30 minutes, or peel, cut in half, cover with water and boil for 10-15 minutes.

Place ham slices in 9x13 inch pan. Add pineapple juice, softened raisins, brown sugar and sweet potatoes. Top with pineapple. Bake at 375 degrees until the potatoes and pineapple brown. Serves 8

Mocha Blast

SHARE Food Newsletter
April 2008

1-cup fat free milk
1-cup chocolate fat free frozen yogurt
1-packet Rich Milk Chocolate Flavor (Nestle Carnation instant Breakfast Complete Nutritional Drink)
1-½ teaspoons Nescafe Taster's Choice 100% Pure Instant Coffee Granules

Place milk, frozen yogurt, Carnation Instant Breakfast and coffee granules in blender; cover. Blend until smooth and serve.

Sweet and Tangy Chicken

SHARE Food Newsletter
April 2008

1-Tablespoon butter or margarine
1-package chicken breast tenderloins (from SHARE) or 2 medium breasts cut up
1-can Campbell's Condensed Tomato Soup (10-3/4 ounce)
1/4 cup water
1-Tablespoon packed brown sugar
1-Tablespoon vinegar
4-cups hot cooked regular long-grain white rice
Heat butter in skillet. Add chicken and cook until done. Add soup, water, sugar and vinegar. Heat to a boil; cover and cook over low heat 5 minutes or until done. Serve with rice. Serves 4

Mango Bread

SHARE Food Newsletter
April 2008

2-cups flour
2-teaspoons baking soda
2-teaspoons ground cinnamon
3/4 cup vegetable oil
½ teaspoon salt
1-1/4 cups sugar
3-eggs
2-cups diced mango
½ cup chopped pecans or walnuts

Sift dry ingredients into a mixing bowl. Make a well and add remaining ingredients. Mix until well blended. Pour into a greased and floured 9x5x3 inch loaf pan and let stand 20 minutes. Bake at 350 degrees for about 1-hour, or until a wooden pick or cake tester inserted in center comes out clean.

Sharon's Fried Onion Rings

SHARE Food Newsletter
July 2007

1-large (3/4 pound) onion
1-cup flour
2-teaspoon salt
1-½ teaspoon baking powder
1-egg yolk
2/3 cup milk
1-Tablespoon salad oil
1-egg white

Peel onion; slice about 1/4 inch thick. Separate into rings. Cover with cold water and let stand 30 minutes. Drain and spread out on paper towel.

Make batter: Sift flour, salt, and baking powder into medium bowl; set side. Beat egg yolk slightly in a different bowl, then stir in milk and salad oil. Add to flour mixture, stirring until smooth. Beat egg white until soft peaks form. Fold in batter. Heat 1-inch of shortening in saucepan; dip onions in batter then fry till golden brown.

Lemonade Shake Up

SHARE Food Newsletter
July 2007

1-Tablespoon plus 2 teaspoons sugar
½ large lemon
Ice & Water

Mix together and shake.

Rainbow Pasta Salad

SHARE Food Newsletter—July 2007

1-package (16 ounce) tricolor spiral pasta
2-cups broccoli florets
1-cup chopped carrots
½ cup chopped tomato
½ cup chopped cucumber
1/4 cup chopped onion
1-can whole kernel corn, drained
1-jar marinated artichoke hearts, drained and halved
1-bottle Italian salad dressing

Cook the pasta according to directions; drain and rinse in cold water. Place in a large bowl; add remaining ingredients and toss to coat. Cover and refrigerate for 2 hours or overnight. Yield: 12-14 servings

Tuna Melt

University of Illinois Extension, Champaign IL
February 2008 (SHARE Food Newsletter Insert)

1/4 cup fat free mayonnaise
1-Tablespoon sweet pickle relish
1-teaspoon dried onion flakes
1-can (6 ounce) tuna, in water, drained
4-slices whole wheat bread
½ cup low-fat cheddar cheese, shredded

Stir mayonnaise, relish, and onion together in medium bowl. Add tuna and stir until combined. Spread tuna mixture on the 4 slices of bread. Top with cheese. Heat in microwave about 20-30 seconds or until cheese melts.

Fried Green Tomatoes

SHARE Food Newsletter—July 2007

4-6 medium green tomatoes, sliced ½ inch thick
1-Tablespoon brown sugar
1-cup all purpose flour
1-egg beaten
1-cup seasoned dry bread crumbs
3-Tablespoons butter or margarine
1-Tablespoon cooking oil

Combine sugar and flour; place on a shallow plate. Dip both sides of each tomato slice into the mixture. Combine the egg and milk. Dip each tomato slice, then dip into the bread crumbs. In a skillet, heat butter and oil over medium-high heat. Fry tomatoes until brown on both sides, but firm enough to hold their shape. Yield: 6 servings

Instant Cappuccino Mix

SHARE Food Newsletter
July 2007

1-cup powdered chocolate milk mix
3/4 cup powdered nonfat dairy creamer
½ cup instant coffee granules
½ teaspoon ground cinnamon

In a mixing bowl, combine all ingredients. Store in air tight container. Yield: about 1-½ cup mix. To serve: Place 1 heaping teaspoon mix in a cup or mug. Add 1-cup boiling water and stir.

The Magical Mustard Seed

SHARE Food Newsletter—April 2008

There is an old Chinese tale about a woman whose only son died. In her grief she went to the holy man and asked, "What prayers, what magical incantations do you have to bring my son back to life?"

Instead of sending her away or reasoning with her he said to her, "Fetch me a mustard seed from a home that has never known sorrow. We will use it to drive the sorrow out of your life." The woman went off at once in search of that magical mustard seed.

She came first to a splendid mansion, knocked at the door, and said, "I am looking for a home that has never known sorry. Is this such a place? It is very important to me."

They told her, "You've certainly come to the wrong place," and began to describe all the tragic things that recently had befallen them.

The woman said to herself, "Who is better able to help these poor people than I, who have had misfortune of my own?"

She stayed to comfort them, then went on in search of a home that had never known sorrow. But wherever she turned, in hotels and in other places, she found one tale after another of sadness and misfortune.

The woman became so involved in helping others to cope with their sorrows that she eventually let go of her own. She would later come to understand that it was the quest to find the magical mustard seed that drove away her suffering.

RAP (Rantoul Area Project)

The Rantoul Area Project (RAP) is a community services program of the Community Service Center—which was established in 1987. It is a grassroots effort which empowers residents to organize, develop and carry out a plan to alleviate conditions that put youths at risk.

RAP assists in organizing residents into committees to improve their neighborhoods and to provide positive activities for all ages. By doing this, the committees help to reduce and prevent juvenile delinquency in their neighborhood.

RAP depends on volunteers at all levels of its organization. Neighborhood committees also do fundraising for their individual programs.

Harriet Cotter spent several years working with the RAP (Rantoul Area Projects) group. Her mother was known as "granny" by many in their neighbor hood.

NO-Bake Cookies

Harriet Cotter—Rantoul, IL

1-Stick of butter
½ cup peanut butter
2 cups sugar
½ cup milk
½ cup cocoa
3 cups oatmeal

Boil together butter, peanut butter, sugar and milk for three or four minutes. Remove from heat. Add peanut butter and oatmeal. Stir and drop on wax paper. Cool and eat.

Dessert Apples

Nancy Brown

6-Apples (peeled and cored)
1-Package vanilla pudding (cooking type—not instant)
1-Cup cold water

Put sliced apples into a microwave dish that has a lid. Dissolve pudding in the cup of water, pour over apples and stir. Microwave for 5-minutes; stir. Microwave for another 5-minutes and stir again. Now microwave again—this time for 4-minutes, stir, and let sit for 5-minutes. This desert can be served warm or cold with whipped topping.

Harriet's Favorite Bread Machine Recipe

Nancy Brown

	1-pound	*1-½ pounds*	*1-3/4 pounds*
Water	3/4 cup	1-1/4 cup	1-1/3 cup
Butter	1-½ Tablespoon	2-Tablespoon	2-½ Tablespoon
Salt	2/3 teaspoon	1-teaspoon	1-teaspoon
Sugar	2-Tablespoon	2-½ Tablespoon	2-½ Tablespoons
Bread Flour	2-cups	3-cups	3-½ cups
Yeast	1-teaspoon	1-½ teaspoon	2-teaspoon

*(Rapid or quick rise yeast can be used). Set your machine to medium. As soon as it shuts off remove bread and put into a plastic bag and tie shut to have a real soft moist crust.

Instant Potato Soup Mix

Nancy Brown—Rantoul, IL

2-½ cups instant mashed potatoes
1-1/4 cups powdered coffee creamer
1-packet McCormick chicken gravy mix
2-teaspoons chicken bouillon granules
2-teaspoon salt-free spice seasoning (like Mrs. Dash)
2-teaspoon dried minced onion
1/4 teaspoon pepper

(1) Place ingredients in a large bowl and toss, shake and stir to mix well. (2) Place in a suitable mix container. You can make individual servings by placing ½ cup potato soup mix into separate containers. Be careful when dividing this mix to get all of the ingredients in each container; the spices tend to settle to the bottom of the bowl. (Makes 4 cups of mix) (3) Add following label or tag to jar or other container.

Potato Soup Mix
1) Place ½ cup potato soup mix in bowl or cup
2) Add 1-cup boiling water. Stir well.
3) Let stand 3-minutes until thickened

Corn Salad

Nancy Brown

2-(15 ounce) cans of corn—drained
½ cup chopped green peppers
1/4 cup diced onions
1-cup chopped tomato
2-stalks celery (chopped)
3/4 cup chopped cucumber

In a large bowl combine all ingredients. If in a hurry use Italian dressing (in stead of the following) and mix according to your taste—into the corn salad.

Dressing:

1/4 cup low-fat sour cream or non fat yogurt
2-Tablespoons low-fat mayonnaise/salad dressing
1-Tablespoon vinegar
1/4 teaspoon dry mustard
1/4 teaspoon celery seed

In a small bowl combine all dressing ingredients and stir briskly with a fork or whisk. Stir into the corn salad, chill and serve.

Spanish Rice

Nancy Brown—Rantoul, IL

1-pound ground beef
1-cup chopped onion
1/4 cup chopped green pepper 1-Tablespoon brown sugar
3/4 cup uncooked regular rice 1-teaspoon salt & Dash of pepper
1/4 cup catsup 1-(16 oz) can of diced or chopped tomatoes
1½ cups water 1-Tablespoon Worcestershire sauce

Brown meat, onion and green pepper; add rice and let fry a little bit. Add remaining ingredients, simmer un-covered for 45 minutes. Sir often—occasionally add more liquid if needed. You can use either water or more tomatoes.

Crock Pot Sweet Potatoes and Apples

Nancy Brown

3-cans sweet potatoes (drain, but save juice from one of the cans)
3-apples cored and sliced
½ teaspoon salt (approximately)
2/3 cup brown sugar (approximately)
1-teaspoon cinnamon (approximately)

Drain sweet potatoes and pour into a 1½-2 quart crock pot. Stick the sliced apples in between the sweet potatoes. Sprinkle the salt over sweet potatoes and apples. Mix the brown sugar and cinnamon together then pour over sweet potato mix. You can use more or less brown sugar and cinnamon according to your own taste and how sweet you like them. Add about 2/3 cup of the juice and cook for about an hour or until apples are cooked. Turn off your crock pot and cover mixture with miniature marsh-mellows. Place the cover back on and let set a few minutes before serving.

Sweet-Sour Meat Balls

Nancy Brown

1-½ pounds ground beef
1-cup milk
3/4 cup oatmeal
1-teaspoon salt
1/4 teaspoon pepper
3-teaspoon diced onion

Mix all ingredients and make into small balls the size of walnuts. Harriet often uses 2-pounds of ground beef and just increases everything else in proportion. This will fill a 9x13 inch baking dish.

Sauce: 3-Tablespoons white sugar, 3-teaspoons vinegar, ½ cup water, 1-cup catsup

Put meat balls in pan and pour sauce over them. Bake at 350 degrees for 1-hour (uncovered).

Cultivadores

Cultivadores/Cultivators

All through life we unknowingly plant little seeds in the lives of those around us. Something as simple as a smile or a hug or an encouraging word has the power to change a person's life. Yet any seed when ignored will shrivel up and die.

And that is what makes the Cultivadores/Cultivators Mission Center so special.

Just as a farmer must work his land and give it the proper nutrients in order to produce a successful yield, so it is for founders Rev. Nelson & Tracy Cuevas and their staff.

Cultivadores/Cultivators is a non-for-profit organization of local missionaries who are training and educating the academically and economically challenged children, at risk youth and Latino families by presenting the Living Christ to them, imparting wisdom to accomplish their integration into the local church and society. Cultivadores relies entirely on financial support of private donations and churches to assist in such vital areas.

In their Outreach/Street ministry they pick up kids and youth in local neighborhoods and transport them to and from school and to their Christian after school program at the Cultivadores center.

They have prevention and education for at risk youth. In addition to teaching awareness of the harmful effects of alcohol and drug abuse the center helps children with school home work, they teach violence education, abstinence education and bilingual tutoring for non English speaking children. The program also offers kids support groups, arts and crafts, and bible studies.

For recreation the center takes youth on field trips year round. They go camping, skating, swimming, sports, cook-outs and other activities.

The mission to families of the Latino Community Christian Center is to have access to health care providers and education including health fairs, preventative medicine and AIDS awareness; to make legal assistance available through logistical support, interpreters, translators and "know your rights" workshops; to build community participation through local, state, and national organizations and local churches; to provide hygiene products to economically challenged families once a month.

For more information or to see how you can help call 217.892.5292 or email *Cultivadores@mchsi.com.*

Editors Note: Tracy Cuevas, Co-Founder of Cultivadores Mission Center and wife to Founder Nelson Cuevas, tells me that this recipe (Coconut Flan) is from the costal region of Oaxaca where coconuts grow freely. It is also a very traditional dessert in Puerto Rico as well. Just as it is in Spain, flan is the predominant dessert in Mexico.

Coconut Flan

Tracy Cuevas
Co-Founder of Cultivadores Mission Center, Rantoul IL

1-½ cups sugar
1/4 cup water
10 eggs
2-cans (12 ounces) evaporated milk
1-can (14 ounces) sweetened condensed milk
3/4 cup shredded coconut

Preheat oven to 350 degrees. In a small saucepan over medium-high heat, stir together the sugar and water; heat until the mixture becomes a clear syrup. Do not stir again until it begins to caramelize, then only gently swirl the pan until the syrup turns amber. Continue cooking for a few more minutes until the color deepens. Remove from heat and immediately pour syrup into bottom of a 2-½ quart flan dish or other oven proof glass dish—quickly tilting and turning the dish so the syrup adheres partway up the sides. Set aside.

In a large bowl, beat the eggs until blended. Mix in the evaporated milk, coconut milk, and condensed milk, and then stir in the shredded coconut. Pour into the prepared dish.

Place the filled flan dish in a baking pan and carefully pour very hot water into the baking pan to reach halfway up the sides of the dish. Carefully place the flan in oven and bake until a toothpick inserted into the middle comes out clean, about 1-½ hours. Remove from the oven and let the flan cool in the water bath. Remove from the water bath, cover, and refrigerate until ready to serve.

To un-mold, run a knife around edges of the mold to loosen flan. Invert a deep serving dish over the top, and invert the flan and dish together. The flan should drop. If it resists un-molding, place the bottom of flan dish in hot water for just a few seconds and try again. Serve at once. (Serves 10-12)

*   *   *

"I am of the opinion that my life belongs to
the community, and as long as I live it is my
privilege to do for it whatever I can."
~ George Bernard Shaw

News-Gazette Community Newspapers

I started working for the Rantoul Press (News-Gazette Community Newspaper) in March of 2002 and took an early retirement in March of 2007 so I could pursue my life long dream writing. Although I have written nearly 200 columns for various news-papers my ultimate goal has been to write books.

Cheesy Potato Soup

Janelle Jackson
Retired from Piatt County Journal, Monticello IL

4 chicken cubes
1-quart water (4 cups)
1-cup diced onions
1-cup diced celery
2-½ cups diced raw potatoes
20 ounce package frozen mixed vegetables
2 cans cream of chicken soup
1-pound Velveeta cheese cubes
Milk as needed to thin

Place water, chicken cubes, onion and celery in large covered pan. Simmer for 20 minutes stirring occasionally. Add potatoes and mixed vegetables. Simmer and stir for 20 minutes of until vegetables and potatoes are done. Add both cans of soup and the Velveeta cheese. Stir and simmer until cheese is melted. Add milk as needed to thin.

Cherry Chocolate Cake

Janelle Jackson
Retired from Piatt County Journal, Monticello IL

1-box instant chocolate pudding (3.9 ounce size)
1-package cherry Jell-O (3 ounce size)
1-cup hot water

Bake chocolate cake mix as directed on box. Dissolve cherry Jell-O in hot water. Cool. When cake is done poke holes into cake with chopstick. Pour cooled Jell-O into holes and over cake.

Topping:

1-box instant chocolate pudding (3.9 ounce)
1-cup cold milk
1-container Cool Whip (8 ounce)
1-can Comstock cherry pie filling

Beat chocolate pudding and milk. Fold in Cool Whip. Frost cake with the pudding mixture then carefully spoon cherry pie filling over top—spreading cherries evenly. Refrigerate to set before serving.

Cherry Cola Salad

Janelle Jackson—Retired—Piatt Co. Journal Monticello

1-can Cherry pie filling (can use one with no sugar added)
1-can (20 ounce) crushed pineapple, DRAINED
1-large box cherry jell-o
1-cup sugar (use Splenda or other sweetener or ½ sugar and ½ sweetener)
1-cup water
1-can coke-a-cola
1-cup chopped nuts (optional)

Bring to boil in a quart size pan the water and sugar. Add pie filling and bring to boil again. In a large bowl place jell-o and mix in boiled pie filling mixture; stir until jell-o is dissolved. Stir in pineapple and nuts. Add the can of coke and stir. Pour into a 9x11 inch container and place in refrigerator until firm. Makes and sets best if fixed the day before.

Chocolate Texas Sheet Cake

Tom Rund-Scott—From cookbook his mother made for him
Editor-Ogden Leader, Ogden IL

2-cups flour
2-cups sugar
1-cup butter
4-Tablespoons cocoa
1-cup water

½ cup buttermilk
½ teaspoon cinnamon
1-teaspoon vanilla
2-eggs
1-teaspoon baking soda

Sift together sugar and flour—set aside. In small pan, mix butter, cocoa, and 1-cup water; bring to a boil. Pour hot mixture over flour-sugar mixture and blend well. Add butter-milk, cinnamon vanilla, eggs, and baking soda; mix well. Pour into large jellyroll pan and Bake at 350 degrees for 25 minutes.

Frosting:

4-Tablespoons cocoa
1-stick butter
6-Tablespoons milk

1-pound (4 cups) powdered sugar
1-teaspoon vanilla
1-cup chopped walnuts

Bring cocoa, butter and milk to boil. Add powdered sugar and mix well. Add vanilla and nuts. Beat and spread on hot cake.

Pumpkin Muffins

Janelle Jackson
Retired from Piatt County Journal, Monticello IL

1-Spice or Chocolate cake mix
1-can (15 ounces) Solid Pumpkin (Not pumpkin pie filling)

Mix together and put into 18 paper lined muffin tins. Bake at 350 degrees for 18-20 minutes or until done

Do-Ahead Breakfast Bake

Janelle Jackson
Retired from Piatt County Journal, Monticello IL

1 to 2 cups cooked sausage (can use ham)
12 ounces Hash brown potatoes
1-medium size green bell pepper, chopped (1-cup) (Optional)
1-Tablespoon instant chopped onion (can use minced or dried onion)
2 cups (8 ounces) Shredded cheddar cheese
3 cups milk
1-cup original Bisquick or reduced fat Bisquick
½ teaspoon salt
4 eggs

Grease 13x9x2 inch baking dish. Mix meat, potatoes, bell pepper, onion and 1-cup of the cheese. Spread in baking dish. Stir milk, Bisquick, salt and eggs until blended. Pour over potato mixture. Sprinkle with remaining 1-cup of cheese. Cover and refrigerate at least 4 hours but no longer than 24 hours. Heat oven to 375 degrees; uncover and bake 30-35 minutes or until light golden brown around edges and cheese is melted. Let stand 10 minutes before serving. (12 Servings)

Enchilada Casserole

Tom Rund-Scott—From cookbook his mother made for him
Editor-Ogden Leader, Ogden IL

1-pound ground beef—browned and drained
1-can cream of chicken soup
1-can mild enchilada sauce
1-small can chopped green chilies—drained
1-pound Velveeta Cheese
Taco flavored Doritos

Mix the first four ingredients together. Place 1/3 of the mixture into a 1-½ quart casserole dish. Top with a layer of cubed Velveeta and a layer of crushed Doritos. Repeat twice, forming three layers of each. Bake at 350 degrees for ½ hour.

Meat Loaf

Tom Rund-Scott

1-Envelope Lipton onion soup mix
2-pounds ground beef
1-½ cups cracker crumbs
2-eggs and 3/4 cup water
1/3 cup ketchup

In large bowl, combine all ingredients. Shape into loaf, put into loaf pan, and Bake one hour at 350 degrees. Serves 8

Fruit Cake

Karen Hampton
News-Gazette (H.R.), Champaign, IL

1-Yellow Cake Mix (Bake according to instructions on box)
1-Small container soft cream cheese
1-Small container Cool Whip
1-Tablespoon Lemon juice (plus or minus)
1-Tablespoon Sugar (plus or minus)

Fresh Strawberries, Blue Berries, Kiwi, Bananas and/or any other fruit

Mix the cream cheese with sugar and lemon juice to suite your taste then stir in the cool whip. Spread mix on cool cake and sprinkle with fresh fruit pieces. Chill and serve.

Mandarin Orange Cake

Janelle Jackson
Retired from Piatt County Journal, Monticello IL

2-cups sugar
2-cups flour
1-teaspoon baking soda
½ teaspoon salt
2-eggs
2 (11 ounce) cans mandarin oranges, drained

Sift sugar, flour, soda and salt together. Add eggs and oranges and beat with electric mixer on a slow speed for 4-minutes. Pour into greased and floured 9x13 inch baking dish. Bake at 350 degrees for 30-35 minutes.

Glaze: (Heat to boiling then pour over hot cake): 3/4 cup brown sugar, 2 Tablespoons milk, and 2 Tablespoons butter

Pecan Pie Bars

Michelle Hansen's Grandma Rita
Michelle is the Editor of the Piatt County Journal, Monticello IL

½ cup butter (no substitutes) softened
3-Tablespoons confectioners (powdered) sugar
1-cup flour
3-eggs
3/4 cup packed brown sugar
3/4 cup corn syrup
3/4 cup chopped pecans

Cream butter and sugar; add flour and mix until blended. Pat into a greased 9 inch square baking dish. Bake 350 degrees for 20 minutes. In another pan beat eggs, brown sugar, and corn syrup until smooth. Pour over crust, sprinkle with pecans over top. Bake 40-45 minutes longer. Cut into bars when cool.

Pineapple-Marshmallow Salad

Janelle Jackson
Retired from Piatt County Journal, Monticello IL

14-20 Marshmallows (1-½ cups miniature marshmallows)
1-(8 ounce) container sour cream
1-large can Pineapple chunks
2 cans Mandarin oranges

In a large bowl add marshmallows (cut in half), pineapple, and mandarin oranges. Mix in sour cream. Cover and refrigerate. Best if made the night before.

Watergate Salad

Janelle Jackson
Retired from Piatt County Journal, Monticello IL

1-(8 ounce) container of whipped topping
1-box Pistachio Instant pudding
1-cup miniature marshmallows
1-can (20 ounce) Crushed pineapple & juice
½ cup nuts (optional)

Fold dry pudding mix into whipped topping; add pineapple, juice and marshmallows and nuts. Refrigerate.

(Real Pumpkin)—Pumpkin Pie

Melinda Carpenter
Circulation Manager Rantoul Press, Rantoul, IL

2 eggs—beaten
½ cup white sugar
½ cup brown sugar
1-Tablespoon flour
1-teaspoon cinnamon
½ teaspoon nutmeg
1/4 teaspoon ginger
½ teaspoon salt
2-cups cooked pumpkin
1-14 ounce can condensed-milk

Combine eggs, sugars, flour, spices and salt. Blend in pumpkin. Gradually add milk; mix well. Pour into a 9-inch pie shell. Bake in 450 degree oven 10 minutes. Reduce heat to 350 degrees and bake 40-50 minutes longer. Sprinkle pecan mixture over pie the last 10-mintutes before removing from oven.

Pecan Mixture (cream together): 2-Tablespoons butter, 1/4 cup brown sugar, 1-Tablespoon grated orange rind, 3/4 cup whole pecans.

Stromboli

Tom Rund-Scott—From cookbook his mother made for him
Editor-Ogden Leader, Ogden IL

8-slices boiled ham
8-slices Cot to salami
1-pound Jimmy Dean sausage—browned & drained
1-loaf Rhode's frozen bread dough—thawed
½ cup chopped bell peppers
½ cup chopped onion
1-3 ounce can mushrooms—sliced
Garlic salt & Oregano
4-slices American cheese
1-cup shredded mozzarella cheese
Parmesan cheese

Divide dough in half and roll into two rectangles. Place four slices of each meat on each piece of bread dough. Place half the browned sausage on top of that. Then spread half of the vegetables over sausage. Sprinkle each section with garlic salt and oregano. Place 2 slices of American cheese on each piece. Sprinkle ½ cup of mozzarella cheese on each part. Starting with the long edge—roll each piece of dough into a roll. Seal the edges and ends and place with the seam down on a large baking sheet. Brush the tops with beaten egg yolk and sprinkle with parmesan cheese. Bake at 375 degrees for 20-30 minutes.

White Texas Sheet Cake

Doug Marsh—CSC Volunteer
Sales Associate, Rantoul Press, Rantoul, IL

1-cup butter (or margarine)
1-cup water
2-cups all-purpose flour
2-cups white sugar
2-eggs
½ cup sour cream
1-teaspoon almond extract
1-teaspoon baking soda
½ cup butter (or margarine)
1/4 cup milk
4-½ cups powdered sugar
½ teaspoon almond extract
1-cup chopped pecans (OPTIONAL)

In a large saucepan, bring 1-cup butter or margarine with water to a boil. Remove from heat and stir in flour, sugar, eggs, sour cream, 1-teaspoon almond extract, and baking soda until smooth. Pour batter into a greased 10x15x1 inch baking pan. Bake at 375 degrees for 20-22 minutes or until cake is golden brown and tests done. Cool 20 minutes. Combine ½-cup butter or margarine in a saucepan; bring to boil. Remove from heat. Mix in sugar and ½-teaspoon almond extract. (Optional—Stir in pecans). Spread frosting over warm cake.

Angle Food Cake (Low-Calorie)

Janelle Jackson
Retired from Piatt County Journal, Monticello IL

1-box (1-step) Angel Food Cake Mix
1-20 ounce can crushed pineapple (in own juice)

Mix and bake at 350 degrees till done. Can be made in an n angel food cake pan or a 9x13x2 inch pan or you can make LARGE muffins with this.

DO NOT ADD WATER TO THIS; ONLY USE THE CRUSHED PINEAPPLE WITH ITS OWN JUICE.

Chili Soup (Low-Calorie)

Janelle Jackson

1-½ pounds lean ground beef
1-medium onion, chopped
3-(10-3/4 ounce) cans condensed minestrone soup
1-(14-½ ounce) can stewed tomatoes
1-(10 ounce) can Rotell tomatoes
1-(15-½ ounce) can chili beans
3-(10-3/4 ounce) can water

Brown together ground beef and chopped onion; drain thoroughly. Add remaining ingredients. Mix together. Simmer for 10 minutes. (16 one-cup servings).

Exchanges: 1½ meat, ¾ bread, ½ vegetable, ¾ fat Chol: 26 mg, Carbo: 11 gm, Fat: 6 gm, Calories: 153, Protein: 10 gm, Fiber: 3 gm, Sodium: 64 mg.

Sugarless Apple Pie (Low-Calorie)

Janelle Jackson

1-16 ounce can frozen apple juice thawed (get the one with no added sugar)
2-Tablespoons cornstarch
1-teaspoon cinnamon
1-two crust pastry
1-Tablespoon margarine (do not use Fat Free)
5 large apples, peeled and sliced
1-Tablespoon melted butter (I used lite margarine, but DO NOT use Fat Free)

Mix 2 Tablespoons apple juice with cornstarch. Heat the rest of the juice. Blend in cornstarch mixture. Add 1-Tablespoon margarine, cinnamon, and apples; blend well. Place in the bottom pie crust and cover with top crust. Brush with 1-Tablespoon melted margarine. Bake at 400 degrees for 20 minutes then at 350 degrees for another 30 minutes. (Janelle likes to use the Granny Smith Apples because they stay crisper after baking.)

Pumpkin Pie (Low-Calorie)

Janelle Jackson

1-egg
2-egg whites
1-can (15 ounces) solid-pack pumpkin
Sugar substitute equivalent to 3/4 cup sugar (Like Splenda)
½ cup reduced-fat biscuit/baking mix
1-teaspoon vanilla extract
1-teaspoon ground cinnamon
½ teaspoon ground ginger
1/4 teaspoon ground cloves
1-can (12 ounces) fat-free evaporated milk
1-cup reduced-fat whipping topping

In a large mixing bowl, combine the egg, egg whites, pumpkin, sugar substitute, biscuit mix, vanilla and spices until smooth. Gradually stir in evaporated milk. Pour mixture into a 9 inch greased pie plate. Bake at 350 degrees for 35-40 minutes or until a knife inserted near the center comes out clean. Cool on a wire rack. "Dollop" with whipped topping before serving. Refrigerate leftovers.

Nutritional Analysis: One piece with 2 Tablespoons topping equals 124 calories, 2 g fat (1g. saturated fat), 28 mg cholesterol, 160 mg sodium, 19 g carbohydrate, 3 g fiber, 6 g protein. Diabetic Exchange; 1-½ Starch

Taco Salad

Mary Kruger
Retired from Rantoul Press

(In large bowl with lid—prepare day before needed)

1-Medium head lettuce chopped—1st layer
4-Medium tomatoes diced—2nd layer
8-ounce package shredded cheddar cheese—3rd layer

1-pound hamburger browned and drained
1-medium onion diced and cooked into hamburger for a couple minutes.
1-package Taco Seasoning (MINUS 1-Tablespoon)—added to meat mix
1/4 cup of water—cooked into meat mix

When meat has cooled for a couple minutes spread over salad as—4th layer—and refrigerate.

Sauce: 8 ounces Thousand Island dressing, 1/3 cup sugar, 1-Tablespoon Taco Seasoning

Before serving—pour sauce over layers of salad and mix together. Serve with taco chips on the side or mix into salad.

Community Members, Friends & Families

"While the spirit of neighborliness was important on the frontier because neighbors were so few, it is even more important now because our neighbors are so many." ~ Lady Bird Johnson.

In the neighborhood where I lived BTF (Before the Fire) I made a really great friend. She would cook up the most fabulous meals and share them with those of us living around her.

Toni McClain probably doesn't realize it but she was sharing more than physical nourishment. She was sharing spirits from her heart. With each dish delivered came her cheery smile along with a genuine neighborly concern for the well being of those around her.

Although she likes her cook books, most of Toni's recipes do not come from a book. She just has that natural gift of making food taste delightful. Her cook books are more for the ideas of what to prepare rather than instruction.

Recently Toni pulled out a few of her favorite recipe books to share with me. It was quite an adventure going from Bon Appetit Too Busy to Cook to The Frugal Gourmet Cooking with Wine to Fannie Farmer's Boston Cooking School Cookbook.

That's right—Fannie Farmer. Just the name itself caught my attention. Looking through this very delicately aged version of the original 1896 cook book I marveled at the vast variety of instructions and knowledge available.

Fannie Farmer was not only a great cook she was a woman with great insight. Born in Boston, Massachusetts, the eldest of four daughters to John & Mary Farmer she was expected to attend college. In spite of not being able to complete high school due to polio which left her with paralysis in her left leg she did manage attend the Boston Cooking School at the age of 30 to train as a cooking teacher.

Farmer was quoted as saying, "I certainly feel that the time is not far distant when knowledge of the principles of diet will be an essential part of one's education. Then mankind will eat to live, be able to do better mental and physical work, and disease will be less frequent."

Anyone with the ability to read could pick up her book and prepare a very healthy and delicious meal from scratch and get an education at the same time.

Take for example her Maine Blueberry Pudding Recipe. She explains that "Wild berries have the finest flavor. If you use cultivated berries add lemon juice to taste."

After all these years off adding lemon juice to berry mixes I had absolutely no idea it was due to the berries being refined. So with that in mind I'd like to share Farmer's very simple but delightful blueberry pudding recipe with you.

Maine Blueberry Pudding

3 cups blueberries, 3/4 cup sugar, ½ cup water, 2
Tablespoons butter, 6 slices bread, and Cinnamon

In a medium size sauce pan cook together 3 cups fresh blueberries, 3/4
cup white sugar, ½ cup water and 2 Tablespoons of butter. Bring the mix
to a boil and cook for a couple minutes stirring constantly. Layer a loaf
pan alternating 6 slices of bread, sprinkled with cinnamon and the berry
mix. Cover and chill in the refrigerator for several hours. Slice and serve
with ice cream or whipped cream. So delicious! Thanks Toni for sharing
this book! ~ God Bless!

Apple Butter Baked Beans

Shirley Stewart—Rantoul, IL

3-(16ounce) cans of pork & beans, drain 2 cans
½ cup chopped onion
1-cup Apple Butter
1/4 cup pancake syrup
1/4 cup ketchup
3 slices of bacon

Combine pork and beans, onion, apple butter, syrup and ketchup together. Pour into a baking dish and place bacon on top. Bake at 350 degrees for about 2 hours. Crock pot method: Combine all ingredients except bacon. Cook bacon until crisp and lay on top. Cook on low 1-4 hours.
Note: On bacon you can fry ½ pound till crisp and crumble into ingredients.

Broccoli—Corn Casserole

Harriet Cotter—Rantoul, IL

1-Egg (beaten)
1-(10 ounce) package broccoli (partially thawed)
1-can creamed corn
1-teaspoon finely chopped onion
1/4 teaspoon salt
Dash of pepper

Mix all of the above into a greased 1-quart casserole dish.

1-cup seasoned bread cubes
3-teaspoons melted margarine

Mix the bread cubes with margarine and pour over top of casserole. Bake at 350 degrees for 30-40 minutes.

Broccoli Casserole

Kay Villarosa—Rantoul, IL

2-(16 ounce) packages broccoli spears, cooked
½ cup miracle whip
2-cans mushroom soup
2-eggs
2-cups shredded cheddar cheese
Potato Chips
Margarine

While broccoli is cooking mix miracle whip, soup and eggs in a casserole dish. Stir in the shredded cheese then add cooked broccoli—gently pushing into the mixed ingredients—until broccoli is covered. Then crumble potato chips on top, covering completely. Place pats of margarine over the chips and Bake at 350 degrees for 30 minutes or until chips turn a very light brown.

Cheddar Biscuits

Crystal Hennigh
Rantoul, IL

1-cup Bisquick
1/3 cup milk
½ cup cheddar cheese
1/4 teaspoon garlic powder
1/4 teaspoon parsley flakes

Mix together and drop on un-greased cookie sheet by Tablespoon into six biscuits. Bake at 450 degrees for 8-10 minutes. Watch closely not to overcook. Brush warm biscuit tops with: 1/4 cup melted butter and 1/4 teaspoon garlic powder mixed together.

Potatoes Supreme

Jane Barham
Rantoul, IL

32 ounces thawed hash browns diced
1/4 cup butter or margarine
1-teaspoon salt
1-teaspoon pepper
½ cup chopped onion
1-can cream of chicken soup
1-small carton sour cream (½ pint)
1-small jar cheese whiz

Mix all ingredients and top with 2 cups crushed cornflakes (or cracker crumbs) mixed with 1/4 cup melted butter or margarine. Bake at 350 degrees for 1-hour.

Sugar Buns

Crystal Hennigh
Rantoul, IL

Heat oven to 400 degrees

2-cups biscuit mix
2-Tablespoons sugar
1-teaspoon. nutmeg
1/8 teaspoon cinnamon
2/3 cup cream
1-cup milk
1-egg

Mix dry ingredients together then add the liquid including the egg and mix thoroughly.
Drop dough into greased muffin cups filling cups ½ full.

Bake about 15 minutes. Let cool about 10 minutes and dip the warm buns into: 1/4 cup of melted butter, then ½ cup sugar, coating all. Serve warm. Makes

Sour Cream Potatoes

Jane Barham—Rantoul, IL

1-package frozen hash browns (little cubes)
1-8 ounce package cream cheese
1-can cream of chicken soup
½ cup milk
1-medium onion chopped
Season with: Salt, pepper, garlic salt
1-package shredded cheddar cheese

Mix cream cheese, sour cream, cream of chicken soup and milk together. Mix with hash browns, onions and seasonings. Spread into baking dish and top with cheddar cheese.
Bake at 375 degrees for 1-hour.

Strawberry Trifle

Kay Villarosa—Rantoul, IL

4-small boxes of strawberry Jell-o
4-cups of boiling water
3 (10 ounce) packages frozen strawberries, thawed
Cool whip
1-cake (can be white, yellow, angel food, or pound cake) broken into 4 equal
    amounts

When thawed—divide strawberries into 4 equal amounts and refrigerate. In a
dish with 1-cup of boiling water dissolve 1-package of Jell-o and let thicken
but not solid. Transfer thickened Jell-o into trifle bowl. Add 1/4 of the berries
and 1/4 of the cake. Refrigerate and repeat these steps 3 times. When ready
to serve top with cool whip. You might want to reserve a few strawberries to
put on top of the cool whip for garnish.

Chicken (or Beef) Enchiladas

Wendy Hundley—Rantoul IL

1-ound chicken or beef (cook chicken, brown meat)
1/4 cup chopped onion
1/4 chopped bell pepper
1-teaspoon union-pepper
1-(8 ounce) can chili tomatoes
Salt to taste
12 corn tortillas

Put chicken—cut into small chunks (or browned meat) into a greased skillet; add onions, peppers, union-pepper and salt; cook for 30 minutes on low burner. Add tomatoes and cook another 15 minutes. Let rest for 15 minutes. Put tortillas in microwave for 1-minute. Take tortillas one by one filling with: 1-spoonful each of meat and cheese. Roll them up as you prepare them and place them next to each other in a greased casserole dish. Spread the leftover meat and juice on top of the tortillas Bake at 325 degrees for 15 minutes. Remove from oven and spread left over cheese and green onion to garnish. Bake for another 10 minutes. Serve with rice of your choice.

Nancy Brown has served as director for the Rantoul SHARE Food program for many years. In 2007 she won an award for serving more than 2000 volunteer hours; many of which were for SHARE foods. God Bless You Nancy for having such a giving heart. You are one in a million!

Who knew?

Nancy Brown—SHARE Food Director for Rantoul

Wesson Corn Oil *eliminates ear mites*. All it takes is a few drops of Wesson Corn Oil in your cat's ear—massage it in, then clean with a cotton ball. Repeat daily for 3 days. The oil soothes the cat's skin, smothers the mites, and accelerates healing.

Dawn Dishwashing Liquid *kills fleas instantly*. Add a few drops to your dog's bath and shampoo the animal thoroughly. Rinse well to avoid skin irritations. Good-bye fleas.

Fabric Sheets can cure that *rainy day dog odor*. Just wipe down your dog with any kind of fabric sheet after coming in from the rain and he will smell springtime fresh.

Did you know that drinking two glasses of Gatorade can relieve *headache pain* almost immediately-without the unpleasant side effects caused by traditional pain relievers?

Did you know that Colgate Toothpaste makes an excellent *salve for burns*?

Achy muscles from a bout of the flu? Mix one Tablespoon horseradish in one cup of olive oil. Let the mixture sit for 30 minutes, then apply it as massage oil for instant relief for aching muscles.

Sore throat? Just mix 1/4 cup of vinegar and 1/4 cup of honey and take 1-Tablespoon six times a day. The vinegar kills the bacteria.

Cure *urinary tract infections* with Alka-Seltzer. Just dissolve two tablets in a glass of water and drink it at the onset of the symptoms. Alka-Seltzer begins eliminating urinary tract infections almost instantly-even though the product has never been advertised for this use.

Honey remedy for *skin blemishes*. Cover the blemish with a dab of honey and place a band-aid over it. Honey kills the bacteria, keeps the skin sterile, and speeds healing. Works overnight.

Listerine therapy for *toenail fungus*: Get rid of unsightly toenail fungus by soaking your toes in Listerine Mouthwash. The powerful antiseptic leaves your toenails looking healthy again.

Easy *eyeglass protection*—to prevent the screws in eyeglasses from loosening, apply a small drop of Maybelline Crystal Clear Nail Polish to the threads of the screws before tightening them.

Cleaning liquid that doubles as *bug killer*: If menacing bees, wasps, hornets, or yellow jackets get in your home and you can't find the insecticide, try a spray of Formula 409.

Smart *splinter remover*: Just pour a drop of Elmer's Glue-All over the splinter, let dry, and peel the dried glue off the skin. The splinter sticks to the dried glue.

Tomato Paste *boil cure*: Cover the boil with tomato paste as a compress. The acids from the tomatoes soothe the pain and bring the boil to a head.

For fast *pain relief* mix 2-cups of Quaker Oats and 1-cup of water in a bowl and warm in microwave for 1-minute, cool slightly and apply the mixture to our hands for soothing relief *from arthritis pain*.

Incredible Edible—Wildflowers

From Brian Truncale (Food Pantry Volunteer)—Rantoul, Illinois

Plantains (Plantago): These common place weeds were prized in years gone by—and are still valued by many—for their tasty and nutritious foliage, richer than spinach in iron and vitamins A and C. The weedy persistence that makes them the despair of gardeners and lawn keeps is a virtue in the eyes of those who cook and eat the very young leaves. A new leafy whorl appears a day or two after the plant is cut to the ground.

Purslane: The weedy Common Purslane, despised by gardeners for its tenacity, can be a rich source of iron and of vitamins A and C. The tender, leafy tips are a quickly renewed and very tasty salad green, and the entire plant makes a good potherb when simmered for a few minutes in salted water. The thick stems can be cut into chunks and pickled like cucumbers, and the seeds can be grounded into flour.

Dandelion: No weed is more successful than the dandelion. Its leaves exude an ethylene gas that discourages competition. A small fragment of its gluttonous taproot will grow into a new plant. Its parachute-borne fruits can stay aloft almost indefinitely as long as the relative humidity is less than 70 percent—which means that when the humidity rises dandelion seeds come to earth.

Chicories: Common Chicory is native to the Mediterranean region, but it long ago spread throughout much of the world as a result of the popularity of its roots. Roasted and ground, chicory root is commonly mixed with—and often substituted for—coffee. The plant is also cultivated for its young leaves, which are sold along with those of its cousin, Cichorium endivia, as endive or escarole.

244

Okay—to many these plants are just weeds. But for those who lived off the land in hard times—these were very valuable food items. I have only listed a few of the many edible wildflowers that grow in our own back yards. For further information—check out the Reader's Digest North American Wildlife—Wildflowers Book. And PLEASE—be sure to wash those wildflowers very thoroughly before taking a bite.

Kitchen Hints

If you've over-salted soup or vegetables, add cut raw potatoes and discard once they have cooked and absorbed the salt.

If you've over-sweetened a dish, add salt.

If you will brown the flour well before adding to the liquid when making gravy, you will avoid pale or lumpy gravy.

Lump-less gravy can be your triumph if you add a pinch of salt to the flour before mixing it with water.

Drop a lettuce leaf into a pot of homemade soup to absorb excess grease from the top.

Ice cubes will eliminate the fat from soup and stew. Just drop a few into the pot and stir; the fat will cling to the cubes; discard the cubes before they melt. Or, wrap ice cubes in paper towel or cheesecloth and skim over the top.

If fresh vegetables are wilted or blemished, pick off the brown edges, sprinkle with cool water, wrap in paper towel and refrigerate for an hour or so.

Lettuce and celery keep longer if you store them in paper bags instead of cellophane.

Brown sugar won't harden if an apple slice or slice of soft bread is placed in the container.

If your brown sugar is already brick-hard, put your cheese-grater to work and grate the amount of sugar you need.

A dampened paper towel or terry cloth brushed downward on a cob of corn will remove every strand of corn silk.

No "curly" bacon for breakfast when you dip in into cold water before frying.

Potatoes will bake in a hurry if they are boiled in salted water for 10 minutes before popping into a very hot oven.

A lump of butter or a few teaspoons of cooking oil added to water when boiling rice, noodles, or spaghetti will prevent boiling over.

A few drops of lemon juice added to simmering rice will keep the grains separated.

Recipe Ingredient
Equivalents & Substitutes

Allspice—1 teaspoon = ½ teaspoon cinnamon and ½ teaspoon ground cloves

Apple pie spice—1 teaspoon =½ teaspoon cinnamon, 1/4 teaspoon nutmeg and 1/8 teaspoon ardamom

Baking Chocolate—1 square (1 ounce) = 3 Tablespoons cocoa plus 1-Tablespoon margarine

Baking Powder—1 teaspoon = 1/4 teaspoon baking soda plus 5/8 teaspoon cream of tartar

Baking powder—1 teaspoon = 1/4 teaspoon baking soda plus ½ cup buttermilk or sour milk (decrease liquid by ½ cup)

Baking powder—1 teaspoon = 1/4 teaspoon baking soda plus ½ Tablespoon vinegar or lemon juice used with sweet milk to make ½ cup liquid (decrease liquid by ½ cup)

Bread crumbs 1/3 cup, dry = 1 slice bread

Bread crumbs 1/3 cup, dry = 1/4 cup, soft 1 slice bread

Bread crumbs 1/3 cup, dry = 1/4 cup cracker crumbs or 1/4 cup cornmeal

Bay leaf—1 whole = 1/4 teaspoon crushed

Broth—1 cup = 1 bouillon cube

Broth—1 cup = 1 teaspoon powdered bouillon in 1 cup boiling water

Bouillon—1 cube = 1 teaspoon powdered bouillon

Bell Pepper—1 Tablespoon dried = 3 Tablespoon fresh chopped

Butter—1 cup = 7/8 cup shortening or 7/8 cup oil or 1 cup margarine
Oil is not a direct substitute for solid fats in baked products. Use recipes formulated for oil if a product made with oil is desired.

Buttermilk—the same amount of yogurt can replace buttermilk

Light Brown Sugar—1 cup = 1 cup white sugar and 1 teaspoon molasses

Dark Brown Sugar—1 cup = 1 cup white sugar and 1 Tablespoon molasses

Catsup—1 cup = 1 cup tomato sauce plus ½ cup sugar & 2 Tablespoon vinegar (for cooking use)

Chocolate—1 ounce= 3 Tablespoon cocoa + 1 Tablespoon shortening

Chocolate chips—1 ounce = 1 ounce sweet cooking semi-sweet chocolate

Chocolate—1 ounce = 3 Tablespoons unsweetened cocoa plus 1 Tablespoons fat

Cocoa—1/4 cup = 1 ounce chocolate and omit ½ Tablespoon fat

Corn syrup—1 cup = 1 cup sugar plus 1/4 cup liquid

Cracker crumbs—3/4 cup = 1 cup bread crumbs

Cornstarch—1 Tablespoon = 2 Tablespoons flour

Egg—1 whole = 3 Tablespoons beaten egg

Egg—1 whole = 2 egg whites **or 2 egg yolks**

Egg—1 whole = 1/4 cup egg substitute

Flour, for thickening—1 Tablespoon = ½ Tablespoon cornstarch

Flour, for baking—1 cup sifted = 1 cup minus 2 Tablespoons unsifted flour

Flour, for cooking—1 cup sifted = 3/4 cup whole wheat flour and 1/4 cup all-purpose flour

Flour for cake—1 cup = 1 cup minus 2 Tablespoons all-purpose flour

Flour, self-rising—1 cup = 1 cup minus 2 teaspoons flour plus 1-½ teaspoons baking powder and ½ teaspoon salt

Garlic—1 clove = 1 teaspoon chopped garlic or **Garlic—1 clove** = 1/8 teaspoon garlic powder

Ginger—1/8 teaspoon = ½ teaspoon raw ginger

Honey—1 cup = 1 1/4 cups sugar and 1/4 cup liquid

Horseradish—1 Tablespoon fresh = 2 Tablespoons prepared

Lemon Juice—1 teaspoon = ½ teaspoon vinegar

Lemon—1 whole = 3 Tablespoons juice plus 2 teaspoons rind

Lemon rind—1 teaspoon = ½ teaspoon extract

Milk—Believe it or not, 1-½ lbs of zucchini, peeled and pureed, will replace 2 cups of milk when baking.

Onion powder—1 Tablespoon = 1 med onion chopped **Onion—1 small** = 1 Tablespoon instant minced

Pumpkin pie spice—1 teaspoon = ½ teaspoon cinnamon, 1/4 teaspoon ginger, 1/8 teaspoon allspice & 1/8 teaspoon nutmeg

Sour Cream—3/4 cup sour milk and 1/3 cup butter or use plain yogurt

Sugar, white—1 cup = 1 cup packed brown sugar

Sugar, white—1 cup = 1 cup honey minus 1/4 cup liquid in recipe

Shortening, 1 cup = 1 cup and 2 Tablespoons butter or margarine

Tomatoes, fresh—2 cups, chopped = 16 ounce can, drained

Tomato sauce—2 cups = 1 cup tomato paste plus 1 cup water

Vegetable Oil—1 cup = 1 cup applesauce

Vinegar—1 teaspoon = ½ teaspoon lemon juice

Substitutes

Brown Sugar Substitute: For each 1 cup firmly packed light brown sugar called for in a recipe, use 1½ Tablespoons molasses plus 1 cup granulated sugar. To make light brown sugar from dark brown sugar, use ½ cup firmly packed dark brown sugar and ½ cup granulated sugar. For dark brown sugar, use 1 cup firmly packed light brown sugar plus 1 Tablespoon molasses; or 1 cup granulated sugar plus 1/4 cup molasses

Buttermilk—Substitute: Substitute un-drained, plain yogurt or sour cream, whisked with a little milk to thin, in recipes that call for buttermilk. Or combine a Tablespoon of white vinegar or lemon juice with enough milk to make 1 cup. Set the latter mixture aside for five minutes before using.

Chicken or Beef Broth Substitute: 1 cup hot water and 1 teaspoon instant bouillon granules (or 1 bouillon cube) can be substituted for 1 cup broth

Cinnamon, Ground (Substitute) : For 1 teaspoon ground cinnamon, grind a 3½-inch-long cinnamon stick; OR use ground nutmeg, allspice, cardamom or cloves, starting with half the amount specified and adding more to taste

Corn Syrup Substitute: For each 1 cup corn syrup called for, use 1 1/4 cups granulated sugar or firmly packed brown sugar plus 1/4 cup liquid (use liquid called for in recipe).

Flour, Cake Flour Substitute: For each cup of cake flour called for in a recipe, use one cup all-purpose flour MINUS 2 Tablespoons.

Italian Seasoning Substitute: 1/4 teaspoon EACH dried oregano leaves, dried marjoram leaves and dried basil leaves plus 1/8 teaspoon rubbed dried sage can be substituted for 1½ teaspoons Italian seasoning.

No cake flour? For 1 cup of cake flour, sift together 7/8 cup all-purpose flour and 2 Tablespoons cornstarch